THESE CA FULL OF GHOSTS

THE LAST OF THE DEATH VALLEY PROSPECTORS

THESE CANYONS ARE FULL OF GHOSTS
THE LAST OF THE DEATH VALLEY PROSPECTORS

by Emmett Carl Harder

Walk with us, share the excitement as we travel faded
trails in this beautiful Valley of Adventure.

REAL ADVENTURE PUBLISHING
18201 Muriel Ave.
San Bernardino, California, 92407

Library of Congress Control Number: 200118764
Harder, Emmett Carl, 1932 -
These Canyons are Full of Ghosts: The Last of the Death
Valley Prospectors

A Real Adventure Publication
Includes Index

1. Death Valley 2. Mining in Death Valley 3. California
History 4. California Society 5. Social

ISBN 0-9713594-0-7 Softcover
ISBN 0-9713594-1-5 Hardcover
1st printing Sept 2001

Printed in the United States of America

Book design and layout by Ron McKinley
Southwest Savvy
Apple Valley, CA.

Text set in 12 point Times type

Cover design by Maggie Heyn, Norco, CA.

Cover photographs, front and back by Ron McKinley
Apple Valley, CA.

Principal Photography by the author and Ron
McKinley

Printing by Jostens of Visalia (California)

DEDICATION

To My Great Grandmother, Emma J. Rich

Table of Contents

PROLOGUE

The following was published in 1931. It is an excerpt taken from the wonderful book, *Death Valley* by Bourke Lee. Even today it will set the stage for the stories in this book.

Death Valley of sinister reputation has a tourist season. The somber valley is on the highway of the world. Its silence is shattered by the distant thud of some miner burning powder in the hills and the closer chatter of an automobile or tourist complaining about the roads. Fear of the valley has been replaced by admiration for its rugged grandeur. Once infamous for the perils of thirst and death that stalked its trails, Death Valley becomes famous for its mad beauty. Artists strive to fix the living colors of its depths in passive oils, imprisoning two mighty mountain ranges and a great desert valley on a three-foot square of canvas. Death Valley becomes part of the America that should be seen first. There are hotels and gasoline stations in Death Valley. Soon there will be hot dog stands. But they will not hurt the hills.

Death Valley is in southeastern California. It is part of the Great Basin of the Great American Desert. The Great Basin is an astonishing arid trough spread over two hundred and nine thousand square miles of Oregon, California, Nevada, and Utah. There are thousands of streams within the Great Basin but not one of them ever reaches the sea. The Great Basin is the land where the rivers are upside down with the streambed on top and the water beneath the sand and gravel. The Great Basin has been a thirsty land through the ages. For millions of years the Great Basin has been drinking the water of all the rain or snow deposited upon its higher ridges. For millions of years every rain storm and snow squall on the upper levels of the Great Basin have sent water pouring down the steep mountains into the burning desert valleys. The plunging waters have cut deep, twisting canyons in the ranges and worn away the minor foothills and mesa lands. The waters have reduced high ranges to insignificant low divides—through millions of years. But the thirst of the Great Basin is unslaked. Death Valley, the deepest trough of the Great Basin, burns with insatiable thirst.

In past ages water wore down many mountain masses in the Great Basin. Then other powers remolded the land that water had worn away. The land was picked up and thrown high in the air. Its rocks were melted and twisted into new ranges. The new ranges were tied in knots to create new mountains. Volcanoes domed the mountains. Earthquakes tumbled the uplifted land masses about. Great faults and slips sliced through the mountain structures and unsupported sections of the ranges settled into place. The reconstructed land was sprayed with colors. Colors of purist, modernist and futurist. Not fixed colors. Not quiet, unmoving tones. Jeweler colors. The gem colors of rock that is alive and changes its hue with the light. There are two hundred and nine thousand square miles of color in the Great Basin. Death Valley, in the southern portion of the Great Basin, rests in the deepest setting.

—from the book *Death Valley*, published by the MacMillan Company in 1931. Page 6, Sun and Scenery.

ACKNOWLEDGMENTS

I want to take time here to thank the many, many people who have contributed to this odyssey. The good guys and girls-and the bad ones, too. As you read this book you will come to know many of them yourself. At the top of the list is "Panamint" (Asa) Russell who brought to the south end of the valley (the badlands) some of the same color and charm that the rascal Death Valley Scotty became famous for in the north end. Right beside Russell is Harry Briggs. He was my friend and mentor, an outstanding character who was mining gold while Asa Russell was telling his stories. Of course, my special thanks to Carl Ruona, a brave and resourceful partner. Without him I wouldn't have had a chance.

Thanks to my wife, Ruth, not only did she survive life in the badlands but also insisted that, at last, I write this story. I have lectured and published all kinds of stories about other people, and then one night when Ruth and I were at Tom and Alice Culbertson's home in Westminster, California, they all ganged up on me and insisted I tell about our life in Death Valley. I had to agree or I would probably have had to walk a long way home. When they asked me what the title would be, I remembered a day in Death Valley when Earl Fox and I were taking refuge from the blaze of the noonday sun. We were lost in the shadows of a narrow, rock-strewn canyon; the shear vertical walls of this defile formed a buttress against the rest of the world. As we rested among the many granite shapes that surrounded us, we talked about the people we knew personally, people that through the years had prowled the wasteland with us, people that were gone now, and I found myself saying, "These canyons are full of ghosts, Earl"

Cliff and Barbara Walker are the founders of the Mojave River Valley Museum in Barstow, California. I'm proud to be a member of this museum. Not only is the museum a must for desert tourists, it is kind of the heart and soul of this wonderful desert community. The people in Barstow have been great. Cliff and Barbara have "pushed and dragged" me through the publishing process, encouraging and ridiculing me till they finally made me sit down with Ron and Kandee McKinley, of Southwest Savvy, to format and prepare this book for the printer. Their editing along with Susan Payne, Marj Odenbach and others have made me look like a good writer.

The people of Trona, California (on the western edge of the great valley), like many others knew the ghosts in this book. They have helped me in many ways. In the old days, Wendell and Vi Swann always gave me a place to stop on the way in or out from the mines, and Vi even helped us once to set up a helicopter base at Harry Briggs's Panamint Valley Mine. During more recent times Lit Brush, Searles Valley Museum, has been my friend and ally, and Ruth and Wayne Payton have put me up and fed me during my many trips in and out of Death Valley, returning to my old stomping grounds, trying to recall the adventures that might interest the reader. Thanks also to the many other good folks who have inspired and encouraged me.

My children, Lynn, Glen, and Gerald, were an important part of the story too. They grew up being part of the Death Valley scene and were often in the "diggins" with us. Even today, they help me prowl around, working on new adventures in the Great Mojave Desert.

Finally, I acknowledge the fact that this book is just my personal recollections, nothing more! Some people might not be comfortable with my memory so I apologize if I said anything that may be wrong or hurtful in any way. The sands of time heal all, fill the dry washes and build new mountains, but may these same sands always and forever preserve the ghosts of the old prospectors. God bless all.

INTRODUCTION

My great-grandmother, Emma J. Rich, lived in the middle of the wild west not too long after the first pioneers crossed the plains. She and I were very close. When I was a teen, she was in her late eighties. She remembered when Abraham Lincoln was assassinated. Her brother, whom she loved dearly, was killed at the Battle of Pea Ridge, Arkansas, in the Civil War. By the time the war ended she was a single mother (divorced) with two small

Emma J. Rich with Tom Harder, author's oldest brother, in 1918 at her boarding house in Los Angeles.

children. With what money she could scrape together, she boarded a train and ended up in Arizona.

Emma and her second husband, a semi-invalid war veteran, ran a boarding house in Hackberry, Arizona, during the period when several rich mineral deposits were being discovered there. I was fascinated, as a child, when she related to me that the Apache Indians would come to her big house to borrow cookie sheets to roast grasshoppers on.

She talked about the Indians that helped her take care of her lodgers and she told me many stories about the miners bringing her gold samples from the rich mines. I found out later that she was well thought of in that part of Arizona and that she was often called upon to be a midwife, and sometimes she filled in as a mortician as well. When she left Arizona, she and her husband crossed the Colorado River in the 1880's with a trunk full of gold and moved to Los Angeles. They built the Winthrop House near the train depot in the middle of the city.

During WWII, I was a "Latch Key" child. Thank God. Being next to the last of six boys, and with the war going on, I was pretty much left to my own devices. It was possible to apply for a California Drivers license then if you were fourteen years old. So as soon as I could, I started exploring the Mysteries of the Great Mojave Desert, dragging my little (3 years younger) brother, Robert, with me.

I think it is proper to thank Emma J. Rich for being my best friend and give her credit for my determination and love for adventure. I hope that I might have inherited some of her skill as a storyteller. It is my desire to share with you some of Death Valley's characters and their experiences.

※

As a Treasure hunter, in retrospect, the greatest surprise for me has been the fact that the most precious treasures I have found have been the people I have met and their stories.

Let's stir up some dust!

AREA MAP

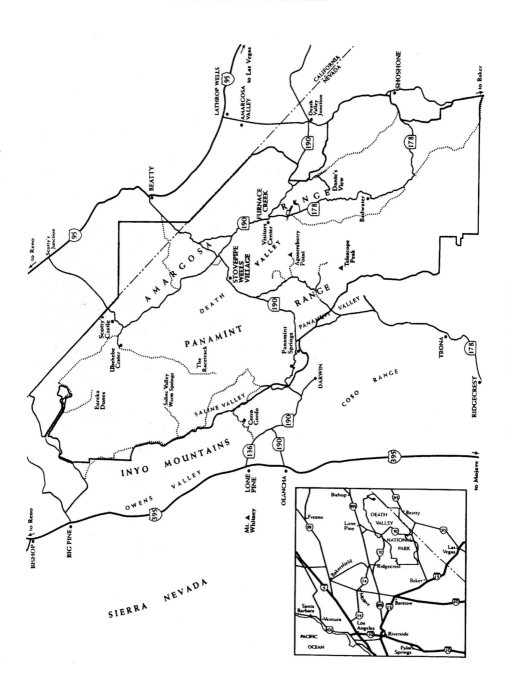

DETAIL MAP

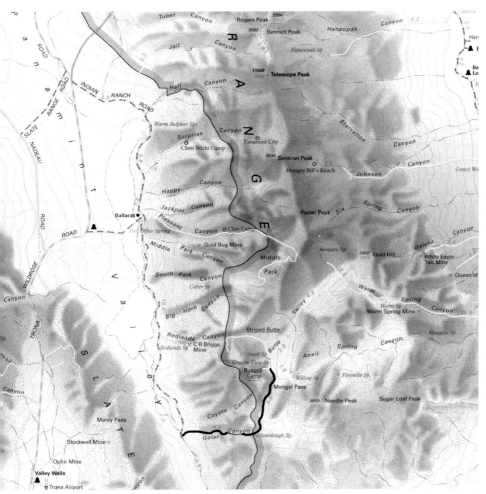

Map of the Panamint Mountains area. The road through Goler Canyon has been digitally enhanced for clarity. This road is 4WD only and turns into "serious 4WD" near Mengle Pass. Map courtesy of Tom Chapman Cartography from the Death Valley Recreation Area map. Complete map is available at the book store at the Death Valley National Park Headquarters.

THESE CANYONS ARE
FULL OF GHOSTS

GOLD, GHOSTS AND THE DUTCHMAN

The south end of California's Death Valley is one of the most remote spots in the state, if not in the country. In the very southwestern end of the valley, these badlands extend for miles and miles, barren rocky hills and valleys, a no-man's land. The highest peak in the southwestern end of the cordillera that borders Death Valley is named Manley Peak. It is named after one of the hapless western pioneers that, by accident, entered here in 1849.

I am reminded of something one man wrote a long time ago about this place, "It isn't God forsaken, because God ain't never been there."

Well, that may not be true, but that's where I was one summer day, practically in the shadow of Manly Peak. I don't remember the heat even though that land can be one of the hottest places in the world. I don't remember the blazing sun–not that day–I was too excited. There are thousands of prospectors throughout the world and seldom do they ever find their dream, BUT THAT DAY I FOUND GOLD! Exciting, yes, even though years earlier Carl Ruona and I had uncovered an outcrop of gold-bearing quartz on the north face of Manly Peak, south of this canyon. That had been near the top of the mountain, 7,000 feet in the clouds. In the clouds, that is, if it happens to be one of those rare occasions when there are any clouds in this bleak terrain. And later we had located where the Lost Mormon Mine portal had been buried, 300 ft. lower down the same steep slope (more later about this legendary mine that prospectors had searched for in vain for many years). This strike however was different!

This was different, yes! All alone now for days; but this time it felt like this was the fulfillment of my childhood dream. As I sat there complimenting myself I began to have mixed emotions. I was elated, but on the other hand, the frightening thought that came though my mental haze was that in movies I had seen and in books I had read where hidden treasure had been found the story always had ended with the lucky treasure hunter and his fortune fading away. Somehow, he or she never survived to shout of their success, and their families and friends never solved the mystery of what had happened to them.

This idea of course added to the paranoia that slowly possesses someone who has been isolated in mysterious places.

I thought, my great grandmother, Emma J. Rich, who was one of the pioneers who opened the west, would be proud of me now. If only she was here. Maybe she is! She could understand my excitement. And so could another figure from the past, the spirit of the "Lost Dutchman." Was he with me? I imagined the Dutchman standing patiently by, yes, over there, in the shadow by that big boulder.

The gold I had just found, hidden here when the earth was formed, was located high up on the nearly vertical wall of the canyon. In this landscape this canyon could be considered a crack, a breach into the heart of a desolate stone mountain. Several hundred feet below me, I could see the rock-strewn wash that looked like a gray banner. What I found that day was a treasure, not necessarily a large monetary one, but certainly a marvelous personal accomplishment. The chunks of quartz that I had pried out of a virgin seam in the mountain, the milk white, conchoidal quartz rocks contained small brilliant pieces of precious metal. The metal that has fascinated and obsessed men (and women) throughout the pages of history.

Many men and women have traveled to faraway places, searching diligently for this tantalizing soft yellow metal, and have not been as lucky as I had been. I remembered reading an exciting book by Hiram Bingham about his discovery of the ancient lost city of Machu Picchu in South America. Even though he expected to, he did not find any gold.

I initially said I was alone—but was I? Probably not! Many years ago, after the first pioneers had brought back gold and silver from these mountains, there were many camps. Strong and brave men and women came to find their fortunes. That was way in the past. Now only their ghosts were here. Walking their trails one can meet these ghosts only if you listen very carefully and are quiet, then you may hear a small voice somewhere way off amongst the boulders.

When you are in the desert, after a while things are different. Is it magic or delusion? Certainly solitude can give you an uncommon perspective. For me, it had been many days since any modern man had blundered into my kingdom. Of course I was also remembering the endless hours I had spent listening to my great-grandmother sharing her pioneer stories with me. Yes, I was in a euphoric mood that day. And of course there was– "The Dutchman," the dream come true.

As a youth, sitting alone in my upstairs bedroom, mesmerized, listening to my radio in its big wood cabinet with a 12" speaker, the voice I heard was the deep vibrant voice of the Old Ranger as he held me spellbound with his narrations of the famous, tragic, story of the Lost Dutchman, his mine and the men who had disappeared trying to find his gold. His story about the "Lost Dutchman Mine" in the Superstition Mountains of Arizona was burned into my mind–I could still hear his voice. Could it be I was now embarked on the same kind of adventure? "The Old Dutchman" (Jacob Waltz) must have been consumed by excitement when he found his gold, so in a small way at this moment, I felt we were kinsmen. I smiled and nodded my head as my youthful fascination about wanting to find the "Lost Dutchman's Mine" came back, like a vision (more later about the Lost Dutchman mine that has become an international symbol personifying the lust for gold).

I had not had to shoot anyone yet, like the Dutchman (Jacob Waltz) did, but there was more to come. What lay ahead?

BACK THEN

Though I had started prowling around this historic valley as a youngster my adventures in Death Valley in the 1950s started as the result of a story about a lost ledge of gold published in a western magazine. This tale inspired me to take an interest in one particular area. After reading the magazine article and discussing it with some co-workers, an old-timer, Burt Chaffee, a pilot that I flew with quite a bit, decided to fly with me to look over the desert scene where someone could lose a golden ledge . We took Burt's old press camera with us, one that used photo plates (Burt had a photo lab in his basement).

This area was interesting for a couple of reasons. One, the story was about lost gold, and two, it was in the south end of the valley, quite remote. We thought this was where a treasure hunter might find all kinds of things.

Out of this area had come several stories written by our western pioneers. In one case, the famous story of the 1849er wagon train pioneers (Manly Peak, in the middle of our map, was named after one of them, William Lewis Manly.) They were the first group we have record of traveling through this land of mystery. For them, it had been a most desperate adventure. They lost everything, some even their lives. There were wagons burned and fortunes buried. It was the survivors of this group that had given this awesome part of the Great Basin the name Death Valley. These people had ended up there by mistake. Now here we were making a grand effort to get there on purpose–our object, of course was the lure of gold and adventure–the same as theirs.

Burt Chaffee and I flew to Manly Peak in a rented 40 horsepower J3 Cub. I had little idea that I would become part of the lore of this mysterious mountain in years to come. Also, I had no idea that our first expedition wasn't going to go anything like I had planned.

The use of that bright yellow, fabric-covered, reconnaissance plane, left over from WWII, was high adventure in itself. Because of the small engine, we had to soar with the wind currents to get over the mountains. This bare bones yellow Cub airplane had a small fuel tank and we had planned to land and refuel on the way.

"Emmett, you've got to get close to the mountain, let the 'up-air' carry us."

"You mean sail back and forth like the eagles—I don't want to get too close."

As we were climbing, I watched the altimeter slowly rotate clockwise as we were lifted by that invisible force. I had new confidence—then I swung too wide—out over the deep canyon north of the mountain (Redlands Canyon). The bottom fell out! A down draft caught us. With a death grip on the control stick, I watched the needle on the altimeter spin backwards like a broken watch. I couldn't believe it, 1,000 feet in a matter of seconds! The fortunate thing was that when I hit the "down" air the plane was headed out of the canyon. Even though Redlands Canyon is not very wide there was room for our wingspan. I was very embarrassed.

"Burt, you take it for a while. I think I'll get the camera ready."

"Yes!"

Mr. Chaffee got us up there, but he flew so close I thought we were going to leave tire tracks on the boulders.

This unplanned air show and the high altitude used most of our gas, but we had figured on that. We had made arrangements with my good friend, co-prospector and co-worker Carl Ruona (We both worked in an airplane repair depot at the time in Ontario, California) to meet us with more gas. He and his teenaged son, Dale, were to meet us on a dry lakebed in the south end of Panamint Valley. On the aerial map we could see the lakebed near Manly Peak, and the map showed a road, a short cut from the highway that went to the city of Trona. The short cut went around Searles Dry Lake and over the Slate Range of mountains into Panamint Valley. This would be no problem for Carl. He said his Plymouth coupe could go anywhere. It looked easy on the map.

When I had shot up all of the film, we headed back. At 7200

feet, in just a short time we could see a big stretch of lakebed below us where we were to land for fuel. The only problem was that there wasn't anything or anybody anywhere down there–just a light brown, almost white, dry lake. The J3 is not very sophisticated. The fuel tank is just in front of the windshield. The fuel gauge is a cork float and a bent piece of wire that sticks up through a hole in the gas cap. The higher it sticks up, the more fuel you have. It was bouncing on empty; the L bend in the wire was bouncing against the cap.

"Burt, land and let me out, then you might make it over the hills." Mr. Chaffee was not at all comfortable in the desert.

"I wouldn't leave nobody down there, no sir! Besides landing and taking off would use more fuel, let's keep going." Mr. Chaffee was no youngster when it came to flying. He used to have coffee in the morning back in St. Louis, Missouri, with Charles Lindbergh when "Lucky Lindy" was flying the U.S. mail in a biplane, before he became a national hero. I turned and headed across the Slate Range. Immediately to the west I saw the sun reflecting, gleaming, off of something.

"I'll follow that dirt road. That's got to be Carl. Let's drop a message," I said. The wire wasn't bouncing anymore. It did turn out to be the windshield of Carl's car that had caught the midday sun. With a large grease pencil, on our only map, I wrote, "Out of gas headed for Trona." My new fancy pocketknife I stuck through the map like a staple to weigh it down. When Burt pulled the J3 nose up almost vertical, I threw out our desperate note. Burt jazzed the engine so the wind from the prop would direct our "Last Message" to Carl and Dale who were standing beside their car, less than a hundred feet below us.

As I headed toward where I thought the emergency landing strip would be, I was remembering all the stories I had heard or read about, where the sheriff had gone out to recover bodies from the wreckage of planes that smashed into some remote part of this desert, or the stories where they never found the missing plane. At least we had left a note.

It was not long before I shouted, pointing off to our left, "There it is, Burt." There wasn't much to see, just a couple of stark metal buildings and decent paved runway. The fragile yellow J3 seemed like something out of the movies, foreign against the rock-strewn light brown terrain–even our shadow didn't seem to belong to us. With our gas gauge wire transfixed in the NO MORE FUEL position, I did not even think about flying a landing pattern as I swung around and lined up with the runway. I started breathing again. Even though I had given up all of our altitude, if the prop stopped now we could make it from here. Burt had not said a word since we dropped the note, but when I looked back as we glided down, I saw he was smiling. After listening to the noise of the engine, just a few feet ahead of me for so long, we were surrounded by a bold silence once I shut off the magneto switch and the prop had swished to a stop. The fabric covered door banged against the fuselage as we folded it down and climbed out. "Now what do we do, Burt? I sure don't see any gas pumps. There isn't anyone around here, this looks like something out of Rod Sterling's Twilight Zone TV Show." There didn't seem to be a breeze, but I thought I heard the gentle thump of a door. We looked at each other, startled. As we walked around one of the corrugated iron metal sheds, we saw there was a door slightly ajar. I pushed it open against a pile of blow sand. Inside the shed we found a five-gallon rusty can with two gallons of gas in it. We would not have tried to use it, except laying next to the can, in a pile of junk, there was a big funnel with a piece of chamois skin stretched and wired over it for a filter. Chamois skin will even separate water out of gasoline as well as a host of other undesirables. Straining that contaminated gas into our fuel tank, we hoped it would be enough to make it back to the airport at Inyokern. I flew right along the paved road and again we probably didn't have enough fuel to fly the traffic pattern. The airport at Inyokern is a large, mostly deserted facility, left over from WWII, like our J3 Cub. I landed on the nearest taxiway, making the rest of the trip, ignominiously, taxiing along on terra firma.

Burt said, "Where's Carl? What's happened–were they stuck?"

"No. It looked to me as if they might have been working on the Plymouth."

Burt said, "I don't think we can get to them in my Nash Rambler."

After refueling the yellow plane and waiting an hour and a half we decided to start a search. Just then Carl and Dale drove into the airport.

Carl parked in the parking area next to Burt's Rambler and walked toward us. Smiling he said, "Knocked a hole in the oil pan, took it off and soldered it up, ya, O.K. now."

"Where is my knife?"

"What knife?"

Young Mr. Burt Chaffee in St. Louis, MO in front of a Curtiss-Robin that set an early flight endurance record.

"From our note–it was clasped to the note!"

"Note–I vondered what da hell you guys ver doing–ya, no knife."

❋

I still have the pictures Burt and I took that day. They show the rugged mysterious and intriguing nature of that part of Death Valley. And that trip was the formal start of our eternal search for the "Lost Ledge."

This is the picture we took from the J3 Cub as Burt Chaffee and I made our first reconnaissance of the area. Striped Butte is in the upper right and Manly Peak in the upper left with Striped Butte Valley in between. Photo by author.

LEDGE OF GOLD

You need to know more about one of the more colorful main characters in this book, Asa "Panamint" Russell.

The story Carl and I had read about his lost ledge was originally printed in the late 1950s. When writing this book I found in my files a reprint of it in the November, 1968 issue of the *Desert* Magazine. I will take time out here to include Russell's story in his own words as it was printed in that praiseworthy magazine.

Even though Russell joined the ghosts of the Panamints in 1970 I can still see him. I remember him smiling as he stood with a straight posture, as always neatly dressed, square-jawed and with a full head of dark curly hair—he was quick to brag about his hair. Often telling that the secret to his coiffure was that he never washed his hair with soap. He was of average height with broad shoulders and he had a pleasant mild voice, you might say he sounded like a radio show narrator. Though I would get so tanned out there that Russell would call me the "Mexican Bandit", he was quite fair skinned. And, oh yes, you might have guessed, Russell was a wonderful egotist.

WE LOST A LEDGE OF GOLD!

The majority of lost bonanza legends are basically true, albeit embellished as they are passed down through the years. Although few of the old-time prospectors who found and lost fortunes are alive today, many of them related their experiences in early issues of Desert Magazine. So you may share their exciting adventures first-hand, we will, from time to time, reprint the articles as they appeared. This one on Death Valley is from the September 1955 issue.

by Asa M. Russell

ERNIE HUHN, or Siberian Red as he was known by his friends, is gone now. He passed away a few years ago and is buried at Shoshone, east of Death Valley. He was fairly well off financially when he died because of the interest he had in the well-run Grantham Talc Mine. [The Grantham Talc Mine is sometimes referred to as the Warm Springs Talc Mine.]

But Ernie could have been one of the richest men on earth and me along with him if—and that's a mighty small if!

While he lived I dared not tell of our experience high in the Panamint Range in 1925, but now I'm sure he wouldn't mind if I do. He was very touchy about it saying that if anyone ever found out they would class us as fools. I guess he was right, but he should have made it "careless fools."

Folks wondered why Ernie, who had mined gold in Siberia, Alaska and California and loved the yellow metal as much as any man, suddenly gave up looking for it and satisfied himself instead by opening up drifts of plain baby talcum powder, as he called it. I was his partner and the last man to grubstake him on a gold venture. I know why.

I met Siberian Red at the Cresta Escavada (summit diggings), a placer property near Randsburg in the early 1920s. The terrain there was made up of rolling, spotted bedrock with no pay dirt, just egg shaped rocks. Although it mined out to a dollar a yard Ernie soon found that it wouldn't float a dredge so he decided to move on. There was no way to make it pay.

We met again in Trona some time later and during our visit he repeatedly gazed intently at the towering Panamint Range visible behind the Slate Range. Finally he remarked, "I understand that four formations meet there at the south end of the Panamints. It should be a hot spot to prospect." Somewhere Ernie found out that a road could be easily cut from Death Valley up to Anvil Canyon opening that area for mining if and when a discovery was made. At Anvil Springs there was a stone house and plenty of water. [Note: There is an error here. There wasn't any structure at Anvil Springs then. They camped at the old stone house at Greater View Springs.]

"Carl Mengel, who has only one leg, says he came through there with his burros—stayed at the stone house and says the area looks like good gold country to him," Ernie went on. I soon became enthusiastic about the area's prospects and offered to grubstake him on the trip and to accompany him, too. I had a fairly successful tree business in Los Angeles at that time and could afford the venture. Before long we struck an agreement.

I bought a truck, loaded it with supplies enough for three months and we headed for Butte Valley by way of Death Valley. In those days there was an old road through Death Valley with a sign post pointed toward the mountains which read: "Butte Valley, 21 Miles." Instead of going on to Butte, the road ended right there in a soft sandy wash where the water drained down to Death Valley through the narrow canyon.

We returned to our original plan and headed up Anvil Canyon making our own road. Every thousand feet we had to stop and drag off the rocks to clear the next thousand feet ahead. To get through the loose gravel we used block and tackle. After five days of hard work we had our road into Butte Canyon by way of Anvil Canyon. The former takes its name from a strata of solid rock projecting 500 feet high in the center of this valley. There was no dirt or vegetation on this huge rock and it was striped with many different colors. The miners called it the Striped Butte.

We located the spring and the stone house and set up camp. We were never able to find out who built the house, but it was built to last. It dated back to the early 1880s and was as good as ever. Here we relaxed for a couple of days, taking short walks around camp.

We had a beautiful view down the canyon to the floor of Death Valley, 20 miles below. The refreshing breeze picked up the scent of sage, ephedra and piñon making our campsite a delightful place.

The country immediately around us was well mineralized. Small veins shot out across the hills in all directions. Some looked like they would pan fairly good and had they been wider would have caused plenty of excitement. The stone house contained some old newspapers and books, packsaddles and odd shaped demijohns, reminders of days that had gone before. We had ideal prospecting headquarters.

We soon found that this was a big area to cover. Naturally we concentrated on the valley floor at first, prospecting a day and then resting a day. We wanted to toughen up gradually before we

Present day view of Greater View Spring Camp. This was where Carl Mengel lived and where they actually stayed since the Stone Cabin wasn't built until years later. The construction of the Stone Cabin will be covered in a later chapter. Photo by Ron McKinley.

tackled the high ground. On these low level hikes Ernie would often reach down to the ground with his pick and crack open a rock that looked like ordinary mud to me. He explained that after a little experience I too could distinguish mere mud from stones that had been thinly covered with mud following a rain.

Occasionally I picked up a piece of float. Each time I did Ernie knocked it from my hand and warned me that it was a bad habit to get into. "Unless you intend to follow the float up and find out where it comes from, don't waste your time and mine. You might have a piece that dropped out of a saddlebag or pack mule. Be sure your sample comes off a vein of ore in place—and a vein wide enough to investigate. Remember, we are 67 miles from the nearest supplies. Don't waste time." I listened to his advice. I knew it was experience talking and I had much to learn.

In time we became tanned and toughened. Our legs were strong. Ernie was convinced that somewhere along this contact a rich vein existed.

One day we had a visitor, a Shoshone Indian—who was leading a string of pack burros. He was on his way to Warm Springs to do a little prospecting. He told us that if we needed some packing in the near future, he would be glad to do it for us.

Another week went by and on the first of October a tall, unshaven man named Greenslit walked into our camp. He was a tough old fellow of 65 and had been prospecting the hills for six days out of Trona.

He took out a piece of ore and showed it to us. He had found it on the ridge near Manly peak in a short tunnel of an abandoned mine. He relocated it and was on his way now to Shoshone to try to interest some friends in his find.

After he had gone the next morning Ernie took the piece of ore Greenslit had given him and panned it out. He found it to run about $200 to the ton.

"I wonder just exactly where he got that rock?" I asked. By the look on Ernie's face I knew he was wondering the same thing. He pointed to the high ridge to the right of Manly Peak. "It must be up there," he said. He scanned the area with his field glasses and then handed them to me. "Look close up there, there's a little gray patch on the mountain side-looks like an old dump—that may be where Greenslit found his ore."

The next day we tried the higher ground. Ernie warned me before we left that when we reached the timberline our vision would be cut down considerably except in small and infrequent clearings. He had me prepare 10 pieces of five different colored rags and told me that should I find a vein large enough to locate, I was to mark it properly, take one piece of colored cloth and wrap the sample in it and number it. The matching piece of rag I was to tie on the top of the highest and nearest tree. A small strip of the cloth was to be tied at ground level. If, after panning the ore, we found it to be worthwhile, the vein would be easy to relocate. I was also instructed to make a note of the general terrain around my find. "This is the best system I know of for tenderfoot prospectors," Ernie said to me as we started out at dawn.

It was a steep climb up the hogback to Manly Peak, but we took our time and had no trouble reaching the saddle on the ridge at the right of the peak before noon. The view alone was worth the climb. Looking over the Slate Range toward Trona the Panamint Valley lay at our feet and at our back was Death Valley.

We ate lunch on the ridge and then made our way to the gray patch below the saddle. As Ernie had predicted we found that it was an old ore dump and there nearby, was Greenslit's new monument. An old anvil and a few scattered tools with rotten wooden handles lay near the tunnel mouth. We guessed that its former owner was an old timer who had found the high altitude detrimental to his mining efforts.

Before we separated Ernie gave me my instructions for the prospecting trip back to camp. He was going to cover the lower side, close to the contact while I was to stay close up along the side hill. If I needed him I was to yell as loud as I could—the air was clear and my voice would carry. If I found anything sensational I was to let him know at once.

We started off and for a time I could hear him cracking rocks with his pick. I made my way around some large boulders, keeping my eye out for snakes, outcroppings and quartz veins and all the time trying to remember all I had been taught during the past weeks by Ernie.

The little veins made me mad as they peeked out under ledges. I followed them down draws, out under ledges and up steep slopes. Few were wide enough to get excited about. Still I took some samples from the widest ones and marked them as ordered.

About four in the afternoon I ran across an outcropping of yellow broken quartz under a piñon tree. The vein, the widest I had ever seen, was about 15 inches across. It was heavy with iron oxide and I figured important enough to call Ernie.

I yelled down the canyon and presently he answered. It took him 30 minutes to find me. After studying the vein he gave me his verdict: "pretty high up, rugged approach, should run about $40 a ton. It would have to widen out considerably to be profitable."

I was disappointed, but he suggested that I put up a monument, locate, and mark it well for perhaps someday the price of gold would go up and then it would be worth mining this vein.

I showed him the rest of my samples, all wrapped carefully in their colored cloths and numbered. He didn't comment on them, but told me that we would pan them out on Sunday. He reached into his pockets and pulled out a half dozen pieces of rock. One of them was cement gray in color and was very heavy. I showed surprise at the weight and asked him about it.

He had chipped it off a vein about three feet wide. The ledge was only exposed for about 20 feet on the surface on the steep side of the draw near the contact. Although he had never heard of anyone finding platinum in these mountains, he wondered if the sample he had might not contain some of that precious metal.

I asked him if I could use his glass to give the specimen a close look, but he had forgotten it. "We'll pan it Sunday along with the other stuff," he said and started off toward camp.

"Did you mark it with a colored cloth? "I shouted after him.

Ernie laughed. "That's only for rookies. An old timer remembers and doesn't need flags and sign posts."

When we got back to our stone house the moon was up. After a sound sleep we decided we had better rest for two days before tackling any high ground again. I placed all the samples we brought back on the high shelf on the outside of the house and we agreed to pan them out as soon as possible. It's a good pastime when you are laying around camp. But we were out of fresh meat and spent a day hunting and then on the next day there were shoes to sole, wood to cut and other chores around camp. On the third day we tended the small garden we had put in earlier near the spring, so we put off panning the specimens again.

Then we had visitors. A couple of miners took the road we had made to camp. They were looking over the country and we spent many hours talking to them around the campfire. When Sunday came again we spent it quail hunting and that night the four of us enjoyed a delicious dinner.

Our supplies were running low so after the miners left Ernie and I took a week off and went into Shoshone to stock up again. We didn't hurry and still another week went by before we picked up the specimens to pan them out. By now over three weeks had slipped by.

Ernie breezed through my six colored cloth wrapped samples and a few of his own before noon. We found nothing to excite us. The whole lot averaged about $25 a ton. The rock from the vein I had called him to see under the piñon tree was the best—it ran around $40.

After lunch I ground up the heavy cement-gray stone and Ernie started to pan it out. He remarked that he wouldn't at all be surprised to find a little platinum in it.

I had ground it up well as Ernie had asked me to do. Coarse pieces of iron may often hold small particles of gold that had to be released if a good pan was to be had.

While Ernie panned the gray stone I sat on a large rock near camp and took some pot shots at a hawk that was circling low trying to scare a family of quail out in the open.

An explosive yell from Ernie brought my thoughts back into focus and I slid off the boulder and ran toward him. He was jumping up and down with glee and shouting, "We hit it! We hit it! We hit it!

"Look at the gold," he cried holding out the pan to me. I grabbed it from him and still dazed peered into it. The bottom was covered with gold.

Ernie was excited and spoke on in a frenzied voice: "I knew it! I knew I would find something good on the contact! We hit it this time, Russ! Our troubles are over! We're rich! We're rich! I never saw ore like that any place in the world!"

After he calmed down he told me that the panning indicated an ore value of $15,000 a ton! "And just think, it's ready money-free milling. The ground is all open for location. How does it feel to be rich, Russ? How does it feel to be able to have anything you want—and plenty of good yellow gold to pay for it?"

I couldn't answer—it had all been so sudden. I walked into the house and in a fog put on the spuds and beans for supper.

That meal was the longest I have ever eaten. It started at 5:30 in the afternoon and at 2:00 the next morning we were still at the table dreaming and talking. Ernie had a list a mile long of things he was going to buy with his newfound wealth. At the very top was a Lincoln coupe, halfway down was a small yacht—he was going to sail to the old country and see his mother and bring her back to this country with him. He was walking on air.

Clearing off the table at 2:30 in the morning I could hardly believe it had happened to me. Then I felt a little sick in my stomach remembering that we had let three weeks slip by following discovery, and in those three weeks there had been a heavy rain and a few light showers.

Asa M. "Panamint" Russell in front of the stone cabin. Photo courtesy of Searles Valley Museum.

Ernie first spotted the 20 feet of gray ledge from which the specimen came while resting on a boulder some where on that vast mountain. The mountainside was steep and the ledge would be hard to find. How much better would I have felt that night had Ernie used colored cloth to mark the gray stone's vein.

Neither Ernie nor I could sleep. He paced the floor eager for daybreak to arrive. He was all packed, ready to go. He had powder, fuse, steel tape, blanket, location papers—everything he would need. While he was hunting for the ledge I was going to go into Warm Springs to buy a pair of pack burros. We would need them to carry supplies for a new camp near our new mine.

Ernie would put up the discovery monument and locate it and pack back what ore he could. When I showed up with the burros we would return to the mine and put up the corner markers.

As soon as it was light enough to see he was out of the door. "Get those burros up here quick as you can," he shouted over his shoulder as he started up the hill.

Twenty hours later—near midnight—he returned to the stone house. Something had gone wrong. His clothes were torn and his face haggard. He slumped into a chair by the fireplace and muttered four words: "I couldn't find it."

There was nothing for me to say. I turned to the stove and started to warm up some food for him. As I did my eyes fell upon the colored cloth on the shelf I had used to mark my worthless veins.

He was gone before I woke up the next morning. That night he staggered in again. Nothing. This went on for days and weeks.

I went along with him several times, but my prospecting partner was not the same man. He rushed from bush to boulder—nervous, excited, cursing and damning the elements that had taunted him with a peek at a treasure and then concealed it again.

I took him to all the places I had marked with the colored rags which were easy to find, thinking that he might, in some way, get above the spot he was looking for, recognize a familiar rock or tree and somehow find that gray ledge again. But, it was no use. His nerves were cracking. He had to quit.

For about three months he remained at Butte Valley and looked for the ledge and then he left it for good. Ernie landed at Warm Springs and got back into talc mining.

We often met in Shoshone in later years and he would always bring up the subject of the lost mine. "Is there anything we overlooked?" Have you searched for the ledge since then?" he would invariably ask me.

Striped Butte in the near background. Manly Peak in background where the lost ledge of gold is located. Photo by author.

My guess is that the rains that fell after he picked up the specimen caused a boulder to roll off the top of the mountain across the ledge, pushing the soft decomposed granite ahead of it over the vein. The rain and the wind could have left that small area completely changed in three weeks. I went back to the city to work at my old job, but every year since have returned to the mountains to do assessment work on my claims. I often wonder how long it will be before someone stumbles across that rich vein on the southwest slope of Manly Peak facing Redlands Canyon. If it is hidden, I wonder if Nature will expose it again for some prospector—more alert than we were—to claim. The ground is still open for location. Folks ask me, "How can you lose a mine?" How do you lose anything? Through carelessness.

Russell stayed on after he and Ernie dissolved their partnership, establishing a classic camp a short ways south of the stone house at Greater View Springs. He had grubstaked Ernie and he went on to be involved in a number of mining adventures in Butte

Valley. In the early days his tree surgeon business was success-ful. I am not sure what all he was involved in down in Los Ange-les. He did share with me that he and his wife divorced and she and her friends took possession of a promising gold mine down hill several hundred feet below the Lost Mormon Mine area on the north face of Manly Peak. She and Russell had mutual inter-ests in the mine.

He had an exciting account of his solution to that problem, he told me, "I was able to get to the tunnel when they let their guard down. I dynamited the whole thing! Collapsed the shaft and the tunnel. Closed it completely. Ruined it. No one has ever tried to work it since."

When I met him at his camp after his Lost Ledge story was published he was semiretired. I remember that he had a job as a guard or watchman, working up to his retirement. After a time, as Carl and I did more and more, and when we finally set up a base camp next to Russell's he was living full time in Butte Valley.

BITTEN

When the pictures Burt Chaffee and I took flying over the "Lost Ledge" area were developed they were great—glorious mountain terrain, geological marvel, naked slopes where you could find ledges and veins. I shared the story and the pictures with friends and co-workers and many planned on forming an expedition. As usual though, when it was time to get on down the road, only three of us could make it. The weather might be bad, my wife's sister was coming, I ran over our cat, and so forth.

Burt Chaffee wasn't interested in surface travel. He would be our air force if we needed him. Carl Ruona, Jack Hamblin (related to the famous Mormon pioneer, missionary to the Indians in southern Utah, Jacob Hamblin), and myself were the treasure hunters elect. Jack had a 4x4 army truck, all fixed up, even with a portable generator plant. Carl would bring his Plymouth. I would trade off riding with them. We had CB radios in both vehicles. It was to be a several-day excursion.

Our first night we slept in a sandy clearing in the floor of the valley. It was a memorable night. I set up a one-man tent, Carl slept in his car and Jack used the bed of his truck. The early gray morning light was so special, like it always is in the desert, so peaceful, gentle, full of promise. No wind, the delicate aroma of the sand and fragile plants, was a gossamer fragrance that praised the air. "Get up boys– It's daylight in the swamp, daylight in the swamp!" Carl was from the logging camps of Michigan, and he banged on a pan several times. I swear Jack and I acted spontaneously and simultaneously. We both fired our six shooters in the air. The loud reports shattered the world around us. After a short quiet spell, Carl called out, in a more subdued voice, "You boys aren't going to shoot me, are ya?" Then it was quiet—for a while.

I woke to a new sound, gentle but terrifying. Flames! I didn't need to open the tent flap, I could see through the canvas. There was a ring of fire all the way around my tent. The new more pungent aroma was the smell of gasoline. I suddenly had new respect for Mr. Ruona. When the flame flickered down, I crawled out. Carl was sitting on a red Jerry can laughing, "Daylight in the swamps, boys."

We caravanned our way around the south end of the valley and Jack had a wonderful time showing off his 4x4 army truck. He could go anywhere. He didn't need roads. He delighted in driving circles around Carl's Plymouth, driving in the sand where Carl couldn't go.

When we finally got to the Butte Valley, high in the Panamints, where Russell and Ernie had lost their ledge, it was a beautiful sight. Manly Peak (a bold stand-alone summit covered with brush, rocks, and high-up piñon pines), was begging the three of us adventurers to try to climb it. We drove to the south end of this Shangri-La, where we left our vehicles at the foot of the north face of the peak. Climbing through the pungent brush and loose rocks, we went almost straight up.

Jack was a little heavier than Carl or I, and he pooped out about halfway to the top. I was making better time than Carl and so I was ahead. About three-quarters of the way up, over a thousand feet above the vehicles, I started seeing fragments of white quartz rock here and there. They were in the decomposed granite, between the huge boulders. The giant granite boulders were ominously arranged in profusion, more and more boulders the higher we went. The white "quartz float" I was finding had flecks of metal and iron pyrites in it, a possible gold ore.

"This is as far as I go," Carl called out from way below. The mountainside was so steep that even though I was ahead of Carl I could easily toss a sample down to him. "Here, look at this—I haven't come this far to stop here—I am going on to the top." The top of the north face as it turned out was not the apex of Manly Peak. The termination of the mountain forms a tee, branching out over a quarter-mile in each direction. The highest spot on the mountain was a large pile of house-size boulders where the branches came together some distance ahead. I turned around and started back down.

I was surprised to hear a rustling sound a short way down amongst the boulders. It was Carl, with new energy. He had scrambled up to the place from where I had tossed him the sample. "Where did you find dis? Looks like gold?" He held up the rock

I had thrown to him. He had decided he could climb farther after all!

We did not find the source of the float on that trip but we definitely came down with the "Gold Bug", at least Carl and I did; Jack wasn't so sure he wanted to try to climb the mountain again. Panamint Russ's Lost Ledge faded away–temporarily.

Our time for prospecting had run out and we had to get back to work in the civilized world. We had outfitted ourselves with several desert maps, and looking at one of them we decided to take a short cut across the south end of Panamint Valley, over the Slate Range (where Carl broke down before), across Searles Dry Lake to the paved highway.

Everything went fine until we got to the dry lake. I was riding with Jack. Breaking trail over the crusty surface of the lake, he was having a great time. A straight line is the shortest route, right? Carl was way behind with the old Plymouth coupe. All of a sudden the big wheels of the army truck started breaking through the white alkali crust, the engine revved up but the truck slowed down. Neither one of us said anything. We sort of held our breath but to no avail; the truck stopped going forward. Jack could not believe it. The engine was roaring, but the big wheels were now just large mud donuts making, a hungry sucking sound as they spun helplessly. The truck settled into the mud, clear to the frame. Jack was gripping the steering wheel so hard his knuckles were white. "Jack– Jack, shut it off!" I practically had to pry his hands loose from the wheel. "Carl! Don't come any closer. We're going to need your car." I clipped the microphone back on the radio and looked at Jack. He was in shock.

Jack said, "Carl will know what to do, I see him walking our way– yes, he'll know."

Carl sauntered up slowly, smiling.

"What should we do, Carl?" Jack pleaded!

"Vel, Jack, I tink you need to put a flag on da top of da antenna–it's going to go down all da way, ya know, Jack?" Jack was ashen.

On the map we could see that in the old days there had been a monorail in the hills south of where we were. With Carl's car we drove down to it. This single-track railroad had been abandoned long ago, the steel rail salvaged for the WWII war effort. The remnants were just one of those desert skeletons, a ghost, white boards scattered across the sand. There were 4" x 12" timbers, bleached and salt-eroded. We could easily break them into sections. We stacked several of these in the trunk of the car.

The lake mud was slick—more slime than mud. Even when we got the truck jacked up onto our improvised board runway, it did not want to move. It just squirmed around, the wheels slipping. We finally got it going, Carl and I sticking a pry-bar into

Striped Butte from near the Mormon mill-site. Road from Warm Springs Canyon can be seen in background just to the right of the Butte. Photo by author.

the mud, and with it wedged against the bumper and with both of us pushing on it, the tires took hold.

From there it was a matter of backtracking to higher ground. Back to the foothills east of the great mud pan that was once the bottom of a large lake. A lake that, when it evaporated, left a concentration of millions of tons of valuable chemicals for mankind to use.

Circumnavigating the sump of Searles almost-Dry Lake, we

came to the pavement for the first time in several days. It had been a rough trip and it was time to stop to look over our gear. Jack walked around to the back of his very mud-spattered truck and exclaimed, "Hey! My auxiliary power plant broke loose. It has bounced around until it's ruined my dynamite."

Carl and I looked into the canvas-covered bed of his military 4x4. We were shocked to see what had once been several sticks of powerful explosives, was now just a brown powder and pieces of wax paper, spread across the truck bed in amongst his jumbled camping gear.

Jack straightened up his equipment and brushed some of the powder out on the ground. He spread it out with a sweep of his foot; "O.K., let's go," Jack hummed.

As we started on the paved road, heading home, Carl said, "Emmett, I don't tink ve should drive close to Jack's truck."

THE DUTCHMAN RETURNS

The next time, we, Carl, Jack and I, went straight to Butte Valley—no fooling around this time. Carl had crushed and panned some of the quartz we had picked up on Manly. There were traces of gold in the sample we had brought back. This time, we were after the "Mother Lode."

With the Jeep parked in the brush (out of sight) as high as we could get it to the north face of the mountain, we started our

Carl Ruona, Jack Hamblin and "Lucifer" in Mengel Pass. Photo by author.

climb to make our strike. Jack Hamblin said, "I have developed a new breathing rhythm that will allow me to get to the top of the mountain twice as fast, you'll see. Rhythm is the real secret." Of course he was much younger than I and a lot younger than the old man, Carl.

While I was still getting my gear together, Jack was already off, "In, one, two, three. Out, one, two, three." He had a strong verbal cadence. He disappeared, going up the sidehill like a steam engine.

Even with the lure of gold, it was still a good climb. Carl and I were struggling in the loose decomposed granite, two steps up, slide back one and we had to maneuver around the boulders as well. About three quarters of the way up we were startled by the sound of a wounded animal, not far away. It was a wheezing, moaning sound, coming from behind one of the boulders. We looked at each other in surprise. Carl said, "What da hell is dat?" We cautiously looked behind the ten-foot block of granite where the sound was coming from. It was Jack, he could hardly gasp. "I...ll —, I'...ll w-w-wait h-h-here."

We found the area where the sample Carl had panned came from and I started digging. Carl had not brought a shovel. He could do magic with most any tool, however he never wanted to be friends with a shovel. I always had an idea that back in Michigan, where Carl came from, amongst the macho men of the logging camps, digging with a shovel was considered beneath contempt. Carl rested, he was winded. I was excited, and started digging trenches. "I'm going on up, got to dig deeper. Where are the chips of quartz coming from?" Time passed quickly.

A voice from far below called, "Hey, you guys, up there! Come on, I need to go down." Jack had had enough. Carl said, "Come on, Emmett, you ain't goin' to find nothin' today. Let's go down to old Russell's cabin an make some Java, huh?" I was disgusted that I had not found anything yet, even more disappointed in my partners. "Christ almighty! I did not come all the way up here to just scoot back down. You guys get the hell out of here, I'm going to get some work in, by God."

They were obviously a bit disappointed in me, too. Down they went, mumbling off into the distance, making a beeline for the Jeep. The Jeep was just a little spot in the afternoon shadows at the bottom of the hill. I dug madly for a while, but then I started calming down. I was over 7,000 feet altitude where it was easy to get tired in the thin, rare air.

Panamint Russell and his partner, Benny Williams, were both away. We met Benny and visited with him before. I wasn't to meet Russell until later. Benny always left the door unlatched—

not Russell, as it turned out. He had dozens of locks he had "borrowed" from Metropolitan Water and Power where he was working as a guard at the time. He and Benny always argued over locking up the camp. Russell carried a big ring of keys. Their camp was around on the east side of the mountain. I was near the top.

Later, Carl and Jack told me they had trouble getting the Jeep to start, but the two mechanics finally got it going. The shadows were turning purple and the stars were coming out when they drove up the little canyon toward Russell's. The Jeep groaned its way up the last steep pitch to the parking area. There were two small buildings that were joined together with a lean-to carport. The salvaged old boards that a desert architect had used to construct this camp sure gave the place a rustic look. It was all roofed over with rusty metal sheets from the same ghost town.

As Carl and Jack walked around to the front door they were talking, "Vel, Jack, I don't know vat will happen to Emmett. He vill, maybe disappear, maybe he vill be the Lost Dutchman. Yeh we might not see him again."

I called out from inside the cabin, "You guys are out of luck, I'm in here. Come on in, I've got the coffee ready."

I had come over the top and down the ridgeline, and as luck would have it, I came out at the right place. Hiking, I had made better time than Jack and Carl had (later I would build a trail using this route). Ben had left the cabin unlocked. The calendar logbook was open on the table. We enjoyed Bennie's hospitality then and many times later on.

Carl could not believe that I had just stepped over the top of the mountain and beat them. They weren't much for walking. My being there in the cabin when they got there kind of spooked them.

Reading the pioneer's journals one could see that they had no problem getting anywhere out here, and I learned the same thing. The trick was, just put one foot in front of the other. After that, like the famous "Death Valley Scotty", I would show up at times and places where people least expected me.

On another trip, just Carl and I were excavating more trenches

Uphill view of Russell's cabin. Photo by Ron McKinley.

(I was doing most of the excavating) high up on Manly, and Carl was telling me I would not find anything, when late in the afternoon I uncovered a big wide vein of white quartz with specks of metal shot through it.

"Let me in der." Carl pushed me aside. The dirt started flying. He suddenly forgot about his shovel phobia. As it turned out, this pocket of gold ore was not the "Mother Lode" and it would have been a lot more valuable if it had been easier to mine, but it was gold. It was good specimen rock. Some of it was very colorful. This was turning out to be a bit like the Lost Dutchman story. Now it was necessary to make sure no one would find our mine. We were afraid Russell or his cronies might; after all, they had been prospecting these hills for forty years. They were always telling stories about hidden treasures or lost mines.

One of the lost mines that they had looked for a long time was a local legend—The Lost Mormon Mine. As it turned out, we were very close to their vanished treasure.

Our clandestine operation made us set about convincing the old timers, and anyone else that came to Butte Valley, that we were there mining all right, but our mine was not on Manly, it was down Anvil Canyon to the east. We filed claims on some old mines there and made a lot of "to-do" about our work there. In the meantime we would sneak up and bring down backpack loads of ore. The joke here is that years later I would tell people where our secret diggings were and they still could not find them.

Then there was a catastrophe at the secret mine. Carl and I weren't always able to get away to go up there at the same time. I had argued that we needed to step back and open up a regular heading and portal.

Carl was thrilled about, as he called it, "Dyna-mite". Any treasure hunter should know how to use explosives, right? It would do the digging for you. He didn't need a shovel.

Carl took a bunch of our dynamite up to the mine and packed as much as he had brought up in the hole. This was great. He had been standing on his head digging down like a gopher. There was a very loud blast and when Carl went to look, it was quite a sight. The high grade was gone, scattered over the whole mountainside!

When we got together again and he told me what had happened he said,

"Ya,-ya know what, maybe ya ought to find the Lost Mormon Mine up der."

✳

It was sometime around then when Carl and I became involved in the shootout at the stone cabin.

The stone cabin, setting out on a point at the north base of Manly Peak, overlooked Butte Valley. It had been built, according to George Higer, by Professor Todd and a friend. His friend was a retired Englishman who had been a sea and gold-dredge captain. His name was William Fison, known as "Captain." Their associate, a Dr. Wolff, had taken Todd and Fison to meet the miner, Carl Mengel, who sold them his Anvil Spring claim for $400.00 and, in 1935, they began to build the cabin.

Captain Fison had camped at the site and did most of the building, with Professor Todd assisting on weekends and bringing supplies and providing help in his spare time. It is a one-

Present day picture of Stone Cabin at historic Anvil Springs overlooking Striped Butte Valley. Photo by Ron McKinley.

room structure entirely of fieldstone except for the wooden roof. It still is an example of skillful masonry work. There is a fireplace in one end and windows on the north and east ends. Through the years it was used by those who were traveling through and needed shelter for one reason or another. As was the custom in most of the remote camps then the door was never locked. There was always some food on the shelf, usually some spare supplies donated by the last visitors. There was a welcome message on the wall and a plea to respect the cabin and leave it in good shape. Through the years people have maintained this shelter, but as in any area there are social (even in this most remote spot) and climatic cycles.

At the time of our gunfight, the cabin was going through what might be described as a tourist season. There wasn't any glass in the windows and the main piece of furniture was a set of rusty bedsprings for a double bed in the middle of the floor. On the rafters, overhead, there were several notes, some fancy and others scrawled in a variety of colors and inks. The typical note said something like this, "Mary and John 5/6/1964, wow!" I suspect that at that time we could have nicknamed the place, "Camp Conception."

Just downhill and quite close to the cabin there is a lonely cottonwood tree guarding a wonderful spring. This is Anvil Spring, so named because early prospectors from the famous Salt Spring Mine found an anvil that had been left here. This spring has been a watering hole for all of God's creatures, I suppose since the earth's crust wrinkled, thrusting the Panamint Mountain Range up into the sky. This green spot can be seen from miles away, even from the north end of this high mountain valley. The dirt road there now, in its almost straight path to the south end, passes right by it. This spring is mentioned in journals by several early prospector-explorers that camped here in the 1800s. They often were looking for outcrops of gold that had been found and then lost, in mountains close by.

Carl and I had put in a hard day before we ever got to Butte Valley that evening; we were so road weary we were not anxious to get to Russell's. City folks regularly made a pilgrimage to his place on the weekends and we didn't want to visit, we had work to do the next day. Besides that, city people sometimes went nuts when they got more than thirty feet away from a supermarket! When we came to the marvelous stone shelter at Anvil Springs, and there was no one there, we decided to stop. We could start out fresh in the morning. Parking in the flat spot behind the building, we soon had our sleeping bags rolled out on the bare bed springs on the floor and I just dropped my backpack on the floor next to me, to hell with the mice, let them have at it. In a matter of minutes I was sound asleep.

Suddenly, within the same moment, there was a barrage of gunfire, and Carl gasped, "Christ Almighty!" We had been asleep for quite a while and I was still reaching up from a dark mine shaft. Carl pushed me and my sleeping bag off onto the floor and then I realized that there were bullets spattering and spinning around inside the stone cabin. The sound of ricocheting bullets inside the solid rock chamber where we were trapped, as you can well imagine, was bone chilling.

Instantly I was more enraged than scared. I landed right next to my backpack on the floor and the revolver from my pack seemed to materialize in my hand. It was loaded and I was crawling out the door on my belly, a' la' Korea, in a couple of seconds. Through the brush I could see several lights and hear people shouting down by the water hole. There was a Jeep; lights glaring at the tree and the water, some people were shining hand-held spotlights in several directions, mainly toward the Stone Cabin! I didn't think they had disabled our Jeep yet, it was out of their view and protected by their main target. I supposed their exercise had started out as a rabbit hunt, you know! But the rabbits must have gotten away from the great hunters and now it was just a matter of, "Let's destroy something. What the hell, we're out here to have fun—beer and bullets, I'm a big man now!"

At that point I did not worry about whether I would hit any of them. Lying there in the brush, looking at their well-lighted attack platform, the sights of my pistol were outlined. The first rounds tore up the ground around the Jeep. Someone shouted, "Oh, shit!" Lights were thrown into the air and amidst the screaming there was the roar of the Jeep's engine. Before I could reload, the Jeep had turned into a faint blur of white light bouncing through the night. No taillights—either they didn't have any or they were holding their hands over them.

The war machine headed toward Russell's camp. As I sat there, Carl called out, "You O.K.?"

"Yes, sure!"

"I guess maybe da rabbits shoot back, yah."

The next day when we drove into Russell's camp there was a Jeep there and sure enough, Russ had six visitors. Some in blue jeans and some in fatigue outfits. Most of them were wearing hunting caps or cowboy hats.

Carl and I glanced at each other, realizing we were in the enemy bunker. Russell introduced us and even though we didn't say that we had been at the stone cabin, the look on their faces gave them away. I'm sure they were saying to themselves, "This is part of the patrol that jumped us at Anvil Springs last night."

Russell had the picture too. His grin confirmed it.

Then, before much more was said, one of them came running around one of the buildings, stuttering, "Th...ere...s moun...tain lion. Up on the...the hill." he was waving his hand toward the slope west of the camp. You could almost hear an air-raid siren, the combatants running and hollering, scattering in a variety of directions to arm themselves.

The broken squad was soon running and stumbling up the steep hill.

I laughed when I told Carl and Russell, " I'm sure that cat, if there is one, is safe. But the odds are that you may have some friendly-fire casualties before they get done. However, I'll bet your cat killers won't extend their perimeter very far away from their beer-chests." Russell nodded and laughed. The old man really did enjoy company. Of course when I made the friendly fire remark I was trying to be funny, but it turned out to be prophetic. There was a casualty at the camp before the weekend was over. Nearly a fatal one.

"Let's get da hell outta here," Carl said. We said goodbye to the old man and left.

Russell, while his company was away stalking through the boulders, decided to give the shooters some extra excitement. The wash to the south of his place was quite narrow and less than one hundred feet away, across the driveway from his kitchen. There he set up a small target for them to shoot at. A very small target.

Later that afternoon when everyone was gathered for happy hour in the small patio area in front of the kitchen, Russell gave the gunmen his challenge. "Hey, boys! You see that little metal thing over there in the crack in that boulder?" Gesturing toward the opposite slope. "I'll bet you none of you are a good enough shot to hit it from here. What do ya say?"

This crew had probably, collectively, spent thousands of dollars shooting beer cans. This target, even if it was much smaller, didn't frighten them at all.

What Russell hadn't told them, was that the metal thing over there was actually a short length of 3/4" galvanized water pipe. He had stuck it into the crack so all they could see was the small end of it. The surprise was that inside the pipe he had put a blasting cap and part of a stick of dynamite.

They all took turns firing and had spent about a hundred rounds before someone hit the bullseye. The big bang startled everyone but Russell. But then—Russell and the shooters were in for some additional excitement. His joke literally backfired. The dynamite shattered the iron pipe and a fragment of it ricocheted across the wash and into the crowd of marksmen. It hit one of the men in the chest.

No vital organs were involved but the fun was over.

FIRE IN THE HOLE

After Carl blew up the high-grade, we started working on different projects. Carl was busy building a resort at Thomas Edison Lake and I started to investigate other possibilities in the Butte Valley area.

Maybe Carl was right. There might be something to the Mormon mine idea after all, since there was enough quartz float around in the general area where we had found our pocket of high-grade. My interest was further piqued when I told Russell that I might try to find the Mormon mine. He advised me against it in strong terms, implying that if certain people found out what I was doing they would, "take care of me." He said, "That mine is a secret mine and if the Mormons find out you are after it they will get you!"

I didn't know whether to believe anything that Russell said about the lost Mormon mine, it might have been just one of his wild stories—and him telling me that the Mormons would get me, well I decided to "take the bull by the horns", so to speak. In order to check it out, I decided to get some other information. To that end I went to see if I could talk to someone in the closest town. I had heard that for local history the best person to see was a woman living in Shoshone, the small desert town close to the south end of Death Valley—not only was she an old timer, it was said that she was the most prominent Mormon in all of Death Valley!

This person was Mrs. Stella Brown, the daughter of the famous pioneer character "Dad Fairbanks". She had grown up in the desert, working with her family in some of the earliest mining towns in the Death Valley area. She was the widow of Senator Charles Brown, a remarkable man, truly another character right out of the old west. Charles, as a young man, became the Deputy in the roaring, if short lived, mining town of Greenwater. He went on to become a developer, mining entrepreneur and a state Senator. As a politician and a supervisor he was said to have been responsible for many roads in Death Valley. Stella was from

Stella Brown, daughter of Dad Fairbanks, and her husband State Senator Charlie Brown. Photo courtesy Vance Gilliam.

strong Mormon stock. She and her family were the founders of Shoshone. [Note: Stella and Charlie Brown's descendants still own the old west town of Shoshone.] I was thrilled when Mrs. Brown agreed to talk to me.

Mrs. Brown reminded me of my great-grandmother, Emma J. Rich, who had raised me and had inspired me by telling me exciting stories about her life with the Apaches while she was running a boarding house in a gold mine camp in Arizona.

Mrs. Brown and I talked for a long time. She told me that, yes, the mine I was looking for was real, and that it had been a legend when she was a young girl. It had been worked from the west side, from Panamint Valley. Something in her past had made the memory of that mine special, she made me promise, "If you do find it, I want you to bring me a sample of the gold ore." I left there with a warm feeling. The Mormons weren't going to get me, I thought (but I was wrong about this).

The search was on! Russell had told me that he and his associates had tried over and over to find the mine, using a whole case of dynamite. He said, "We finally decided that we would have to wait till they invented a more powerful explosive. During World War II, I even tried to get some soldier boys to fly over and drop a big bomb." I also heard his stories about their nightly card games and the still they used to have under the trap door in the floor of their tent; these things might have interfered with them finding the Mormon diggings.

There had to be a better way to look for this lost mine. I would set up a camp near the top of the Manly Peak, close to the area where the mine was supposed to be. There social activities would not distract me. We could celebrate if, and after, I found the mine.

Providence was on my side. Just then three young people, two men and a woman, arrived in camp. They were college students on vacation. They were stuck in Butte Valley when they knocked a hole in the oil pan of their Volkswagen Bug. Clinton Anderson, living at Greater View Spring, had contracted to repair the car, but he told them. "It may take me a few days to solder up that hole." Well, as luck would have it these visitors wanted to get to the top of Manly Peak. As it turned out the one man's father was Brad Johnson, the geologist who had created the Manly Peak geological quadrangle map of the area and had written the report I was using. [Note: I had contacted Brad Johnson and he had sent me copies of his geological study of the area.] The son wanted to be able to tell his dad that he had climbed to the top of "his dad's mountain". The men were both in great physical shape as they had been paying there way through college by working in Canada as Smoke Jumpers, the men who, during the fire season, parachute in to fight forest fires. I made a deal with them. I would pay them and guide them to the top of the mountain if they would help me pack supplies up there for my high camp.

The four of us, and a burro made the trip. The Johnson boy's girl friend rode on the burro and the rest of us had heavily loaded backpacks. We had a great time, and I was all set to stay up top (when I did get back to the base camp I found the money I had paid them in my refrigerator with a thank you note).

After several days work at high altitude without any results I began to think maybe Russ was right.

The big boulders there were not too hard to move because the slope was so steep—just a little dynamite nudge and they would roll out of the way. Gravity was on my side. In most places, it was only three or four feet to bedrock. Julie, one of Russ's burros I had used to set up my high camp, had packed a six-foot-long pry bar up to the diggings for me. Finally, I started driving the bar in with a double-jack hammer till I hit bedrock. Soon I had the outline of a depression, about the right size for the portal

This is Julie with two friends, Carl Ruona and Jack Hamblin in the background. Photo by author.

of a tunnel. Trenching there, I found a wet layer of decomposed granite. Not wanting to push my luck, having been up on the mountain for several days, it was time to go down to base camp and see if I could find someone to help me. I needed someone to be a witness. Someone to be there if I did open up a tunnel, to tell where to look for my body if something went wrong.

On the way to camp, to my surprise, I met a solitary prospector, a young man. Prospecting alone isn't a smart thing to do,

Lone prospector "Jim" on top of Manly Peak. We opened the Lost Mormon Mine. Photo by author.

very dangerous. (I have done it many times, but that's different.) When he said, "I have come out alone. My friends at work laugh at me, but I'm going to find something, I'll show them."

Well! Here was my man. We went on down to camp. After talking to him over camp stew, I figured I could trust him.

He was a stout fellow, about six feet, brown hair, could have played in a John Ford movie.

"If you will work with me one day, Jim, I will take you to a spot on the mountain where you can fill your pack with gold ore samples." (Carl missed some.) Jim readily agreed. Before it was light, we started up the mountain. We both had backpacks, shovels, and a six-gun. We were ready for anything.

It was still early morning. First we went to the old diggings (the Carl Ruona bomb crater). Jim filled his pack about half full. One of the pieces, which he broke with his rock hammer, was one of the largest pieces of gold I had seen from there. We made our way down (it was only three hundred feet below) to the new diggings. I had already moved a lot of dirt and boulders. Jim and I worked steady and by late afternoon we had made a good-sized dent in the mountain.

This had all been a dream—Then my shovel broke through, into the top arch of a tunnel.

I sat back, "Jim, old Howard Carter (the man who opened King Tut's Tomb) must have felt a little bit like I feel right now." What a thrill! If I had any idea what was to come, it probably would have been prudent to have covered it back up again, right then.

When I crawled in the small opening I had made, just inside the portal, there was a stash of select high-grade ore waiting for me—that someone, a long time ago, had stacked up there neatly against the side of the tunnel. Who the culprit was (in Egyptian days it would have been a grave robber) we'll talk about later in another chapter. This ore had apparently been left in the mine by someone in there working later, after it had originally been sealed up.

The Lost Mormon Mine. We had opened it up; the locals had been dreaming, making up stories about it for over three decades!

We took turns using a candle to test for bad air (I'm sure glad there wasn't any flammable methane gas present). The tunnel was 180 feet deep. Unlike Russell's legend, the sides were not wallboard-smooth, except for the clay-like slick sides of the faulting, the hanging wall. There were no tools, just a tin-can miner's candle-lamp in the back of the tunnel. Near the end of the tunnel there was a raise (vertical shaft) that twisted up to some dark place out of the range of our feeble light. There had been a series of cross-timbers in the raise, but they had rotted away and were just a large pile of limp rag-like fibers on the floor of the tunnel now.

Jim had something to show his co-workers now and a story to tell—who would believe him? He promised not to tell where he had found his pocket of gold. I don't know what happened. I never saw him again. He was a big help and I'm grateful. I hope nothing ominous happened to him.

Russell didn't believe I had opened the mine. I continued working on the (two-mile) trail I had built from Russell's camp to the Lost Mormon Mine. Working alone on that trail, I really enjoyed myself. The weather was just perfect. The view was beyond description.

Russell did not believe, but Carl did, and he came as soon as he got word. We had a real honest-to-goodness mine, so what if it was high up on Manly Peak, on top of the world.

BUTTE VALLEY BANDITS

Let me interrupt long enough to add this tale.

Around 1967, just before we opened the Lost Mormon Mine, Russell had an exciting encounter with bandits.

I was staying in the trailer that Carl and I had set up next to Russell's camp. Carl was not there. At the first light the morning after this had happened Russell woke me up banging on the frail tin-covered door. He was all excited.

He told me that it had been a very dark night and just as he came up to the upper end of Warm Springs Canyon, ready to

A modern facility at Russell's camp. Photo by Ron McKinley.

enter Butte Valley, he saw the lights of a vehicle coming towards him some distance ahead. He said, "Since there is no place to pass there in that rocky stretch of the road ahead of me I pulled off at the intersection of the mine road that takes off towards Arrastre Springs, to the north. We call that spot the Sign Post, the old post there once had a sign on it.

"Well, I waited there quite a while and no car came on, and I didn't see any lights anymore. So I fired up the old van and went on. I didn't meet anyone and then by God lights came on right behind me! I sped up and so did they. The chase was on.

"I knew they were some kind of bandits and they were after me. I of course knew the road a hell of a lot better than they did. I was able to pull right away from them, Christ, I don't know where they came from—all of a sudden there they were."

He said that on his way back from Las Vegas he had stopped at the Crow Bar, the grill and saloon in Shoshone. "Someone there that knew where I was going must have gone on ahead and got set up to ambush me. Boy, I sure left them in the dust, they may have wrecked. I looked up the valley with a telescope in the twilight but I wasn't able to see any vehicle around anywhere. Their lights quit somewhere near the Stone Cabin at Anvil Springs. I don't know what happened to them, but I think I broke a main leaf in the right rear spring on my old van.

"When I got here last night I kept my lights off, and I went into the house and got my revolver loaded. Just in case they knew their way around here I hiked across from the kitchen to the other side of the wash and hid in the boulders there. If they had come on in I would have had a big surprise for them."

This was the most excitement he had had in a long time and as his weekend visitors began showing up this became quite a tale. He told it over and over.

❋

To begin with I was a bit angry when Russell told me about him hiding out in the rocks waiting to shoot someone. You see I had walked into camp after he had set up his own ambush site. It was a wonder he didn't shoot me.

I knew that he had come back from town and as I walked up

the drive I expected to see lights and when I didn't I guessed wrongly that he must have stopped off next door at Greater View Springs to visit with the Andersons. What might have saved me was that I didn't have a flashlight, walking in the dark he could not see me very well, and I was whistling as I trudged up the hill and into camp. Little did I suspect that close by there was a local bandit, Russell, hiding in the rocks. If he was where he said he was he had to have heard me, and since the dog did not bark he would have realized it was me.

Unaware that I was in peril I went around and fed the burros at the corral and then went up to his cabin—over to the kitchen, where his dog was tied and fed him. When I had the chores done I whistled my way over to our trailer and turned in. I had had a hard day. All that time Russell was there and he never stepped out to warn me that he was expecting a gang of bandits to slink their way over the hill to rob and murder us.

Yes, I was angry! By then I had known Russell long enough I could pretty well guess why he kept quiet. He figured that if the

View of Russell's camp showing the kitchen and the honeymoon apartments are behind in the background. Photo by Ron McKinley.

bad guys did come they would confront me. And "devil take the hind most" as they say. I didn't think Russell was very brave— but I knew he was smart—he planned to be around to write the story!

There also was quite a bit about the Butte Valley bandits he didn't know, but I did know. However I was reluctant to tell him all that I knew. His bandits were still around, in fact, quite close at hand.

The next day when Russell and I were there alone I went over to talk to him. We sat at the local conference table; the round kitchen table in the cook shack. As we sat enjoying a cup of coffee I tried to tell him the other side of the story without damaging his ego too much.

I said, "You know what Russell, I don't think you ought to tell that bandit story of yours any more."

"Why not?" he retorted.

"Well, let me tell you what really happened."

"Early that day Ballarat Bob had driven up from the Barker camp and stopped by here. He was driving that army four-wheel drive truck of his. He and I went over to visit the two guys and a girl that had broke down and were staying at the stone cabin at Anvil Springs (The Smoke Jumpers in the earlier chapter). They were waiting for Clinton Anderson to repair their little Volkswagen bug.

"After talking with them for a while I told them that if they were game I would lead them to the mysterious Spanish style arrastré at a spring in the very north end of Butte Valley. They all thought it was a great chance for adventure and Bob, though he had not been to this spot before, knew that the arrastré was supposed to be the key to a lost gold mine story.

"Bob drove us up to where the road turns to the east and then he took off cross-country up onto the great brush covered alluvium fans that spill down from the higher peaks above the valley. As we got closer to the mountain wall the terrain became so rocky that we had to leave the truck and walk. We soon came to an old Indian trail and it headed toward the spring. It soon became apparent that we were going to run out of daylight, the shadows of the high Panamints began to surround us. Reluctantly we headed back, I would take them there some other day. There was a road that would take us almost to the spring, but Bob had wanted to show off his army truck. By the time we got back to his "gem" it was getting pretty dark. Bob headed off in the general direction of the road but the going wasn't easy. Sometimes we had to get out and move some rocks. His lights weren't very bright but we did all right.

Author's Army Dodge truck near Greater View Camp. Photo by author.

"Then we saw car lights coming up from Warm Springs Canyon and we guessed that it was probably you. All of us had been out of touch for a while and wanted to hear some news, any news! We came to a bluff over the road. It was very steep and the slope was covered with a few large rocks. We could still see the lights coming but we had to move the rocks out of the way to get on the road. We hurried, Bob shut off the truck and got out too, and as the four of us were clearing the way you came driving up. We thought you would see us and I ran toward the road waving and hollering. But I guess you were going so fast the truck was making too much noise.

"We laughed and I said, "Maybe he has brought a woman back with him and he doesn't want to talk to us." So that was when the lights appeared in the road behind you. We ran back to Bob's truck and rolled down the slope and were on the road close behind you. Bob flashed the light and we were surprised when you took off like a bat out of hell. We tried to catch you but you kept going faster. I said to Bob, "Back off before we all crash."

"We stopped, just like you said, at the stone cabin. The three stranded adventurers got out there. Bob let me out when he came to your road and I walked to camp.

"Thanks for not shooting me."

Russell was not amused at all. He loved to get the laugh on someone but when he was embarrassed it was a different story. Anyway, after that he did not tell anyone about the bandits, not while I was around, but he did have another tale though, an even better one, about Mexican bandits stalking his camp years before. I think he got that one published in the *Desert Magazine.*

As I look back on it I feel a bit ashamed for wrecking his car chase story. The amazing thing, I thought, was he had told a true story, every detail accurate, except that there weren't any bad guys.

And later when I heard what had happened before we had tried to stop Russell on the road I could better understand his dilemma. I happened to talk to someone who had been at the Crow Bar saloon when Russell had stopped on his way home that night. Russell always enjoyed carrying on like one of the valley's greatest con men, Death Valley Scotty. He would ordinarily put on some kind of a show when he stopped by the saloon. He usually left after he would make out like he was a man of mystery. And that night he had overplayed his hand. Before he had gone to town I had asked him to act as an agent for me to buy some mining claims. His cut of the deal had left him with a modest stack of money. The guy I talked to told me that Russell had sat there in the saloon with a stack of twenty-dollar bills on the bar in front of him. He had them long edge down, fanning them back and forth like a deck of cards. Of course he never let on where the money came from or how much was there. I suppose that after he left the Crow Bar he realized what a dumb stunt he had pulled. I could imagine that he was pretty nervous when he got on that lonely dirt road into the badlands. Asa Russell often had luck on his side and under the circumstances there could have damned well been someone waiting for him.

THE HIT MEN

It was back down to the city to tool up for a mine that wasn't easy to get to. Carl would arrange to have pack animals shipped down from the High Sierras (It was winter time and we would only have to pay trucking and feed.) My wife and I went to work in a hanger at the Rialto Airport, welding up posts for a corral and a couple of hitching rails, too.

When we got everything together Carl and I headed back to the mine.

On the way that time we met a new Death Valley character—"One Arm" Anderson. He was certainly one of the special personalities that we met during our adventure with the Lost Mormon Mine. We were in a World War II type Jeep, built for the badlands. The Jeep had no doors, military issue except for a metal top and a coat of red paint. Carl called it "Lucifer".

It was late in the afternoon as we went through the mining town of Trona on the west side of Death Valley when we stopped at the grocery store for a last minute catch-up of victuals for the camp. When we left the parking lot, Carl was driving and I saw an old flatbed Chevy truck with a bulging load of salvaged lumber. It was parked in front of a liquor store on our side of the street, just beyond the parking lot. Coming out of the store was a large man with a ruddy complexion and full head of dark curly hair. He was tall, well built, but only had one arm. He was wearing a blue denim shirt with one short sleeve and pin-striped suit pants. Grasped firmly in his only hand was a paper sack that snugly concealed what looked like a quart bottle.

Days before when we had last talked with Russell at his camp, he had asked us to keep our eye out on our way back for a friend of his, "One Arm" Anderson. He explained that Mr. Anderson owned the tree surgeon business that he, Russell, once had, and that Anderson was going to be bringing up to Russell's camp a truck load of lumber for new construction.

I had not expected to find anyone trying to bring a truckload of anything in from the west side, at least not the way we were

going. We were going to go up through the famous Goler Wash
(Goler Canyon on maps and often confused with Goller Canyon
near Randsburg. Gold was discovered in both these locations in
1849.) in the south end of the Panamint Mountains. Most of the
time, this wash was barely fit for pack animals. The narrow road
twisted and lurched up over thirteen waterfalls in what could be
described as a crack in the mountain, in places not quite wide

Photo of Goler Wash in the early 1970s. Photo by author.

enough for the Jeep. Going in this way was an adventure all by
itself. Not the least of the grandeur of the trip was the fact that the
canyon walls go straight up over a thousand feet on either side,
and you get the sensation that you are inside the mountain.

I asked Carl to stop and see if the big guy was really the

Anderson that Russell had talked about. We pulled up beside the truck and as I got out of the Jeep the big guy came over to me. He said, "Hello there, what the hell can I do for you?"

I asked him if he was Mr. Anderson. "Yes, I am, and who in hell are you guys?" I introduced Carl and myself and said, "We are friends of Russell." "Are you boys going in through Goler Wash by any chance?" he asked. "Yes, we are," Carl told him.

"Well now, that is great. How about if I ride in with you guys and check the road out, O.K.?" Carl nodded his head.

"Great, just let me tell my young swamper, Gene, what I'm going to do and I'll be right back, O.K.?" Carl nodded his head again and the big man spun around and talked to Gene, who was waiting in the truck. When he finished, he came back and deftly climbed into the Jeep with us crowding Carl and me over. Fortunately neither Carl nor I were too broad of beam back then.

Trona is a special mining town isolated by itself in a stark valley by a large dry lake in the high desert. There they produce most of the potash and a lot of other chemicals for the whole USA. The valley there is filled with the chemical smell of sulphur dioxide. The fresh desert air was refreshing when we topped the Slate Range north of Trona and started descending into Panamint Valley on the winding two-lane asphalt road.

I was surprised by Anderson's dexterity with his one hand. Holding the bottle between his legs he uncapped it, threw the cap away and held the bottle toward us. "You boys like a little snort of 'Who hit John'?"

Anderson was more than disappointed when we declined. In fact, he was insulted and suspicious. After all, who could trust a man that would turn down good whiskey. He said gruffly, "I guess I should have kept the cap."

By the time we started down into Panamint Valley, Anderson had lowered the whiskey level. That was necessary, as we all knew there was quite a bit of bumpy road ahead.

I was becoming a bit worried about our passenger falling out on the turns. He held the sacked whiskey bottle as if his life depended on it and he could not brace himself. He leaned dangerously out of the Jeep on the left-hand turns.

It was getting dark when we got to the floor of the valley and started across the dry lake toward the ghost town of Ballarat. There was enough light left to see the outlines of the town's deserted adobe ruins. There were a few cars around one building, but there were no lights on there.

Anderson said, "We are not going the right way!"

"Yes we are, Ballarat may look different to you now, I guess. Some squatters have moved in there lately."

As Carl turned south out of the ghostly buildings and started down the road skirting the dry lake we could smell the salt mud flats. Drainage from the high mountains on our left spilled out onto the lakebed forming dark colored fans. We would have a level road for several miles before we had to turn up the alluvium and into Goler Wash.

The moonlight silhouetted the creosote brush and made the lakebed glow as we moved stealthily into the dark. The Jeep's dim lights seemed out of place.

This was usually the best part of the trip for me, but not this night.

Anderson said, "Damn it! I've been to Russell's camp before, and this sure as hell is not the way!" He emphasized his statement by taking a big draft of whiskey from his bottle. "We are doing just fine, sit back and relax," I said.

Halfway to Goler Wash he began to sob, "I don't know why you are doing this—I never hurt you guys. You guys have been hired to do this, I know. You are going to shoot me, aren't you?"

"You're out of your blooming mind, Anderson," I said. He didn't hear me. As far as he was concerned, he was way into that downward spiral, committed, this was the end. We could not change his mind; try as we would.

Carl started to maneuver up the dry rocky waterfalls in Goler wash. Lucifer was bouncing in every direction. The tires were vibrating violently, spinning, searching for traction, and there was the smell of scorched rubber. It was bad enough, but Anderson's moaning and carrying on made it really bad, plus all the time I was holding on to him to keep him from falling out.

By the time we arrived at Russell's camp, I was worn out.

Our puny headlights arced their way into the parking area. The dim glow outlined the shacks made of old lumber from the silent mining camps.

"By God, this...ss...ish Russell's, by God, it isshh. You boysh ish all right after all". Then, just as I let out a sigh of relief, Anderson climbed out of the Jeep and fell over the edge of the hill! "Ohhhhhhh————" we heard, as he dropped away into the black night. "Jesus! Carl get the flashlight!"

The light had been on in the kitchen when we drove in, and Russell came out with a lantern, "What in the hell is going on out here!"

I said. "It's your friend Anderson, Russ, he went over the edge." Carl came around with his light and Russell and he lit up the slope. Halfway down there was one scrawny sapling. Anderson's arm was wrapped around it and he still had a firm grip on the whiskey bottle.

It took the three of us to get him to the shack. As soon as he hit the bed he was snoring loudly. We all let out a sigh.

View showing the "dead battery road" driveway into Russell's camp where "One Arm" Anderson fell over the side of the hill. Photo by Ron McKinley.

It was very quiet and peaceful that night until some wild burros came over into the camp and woke us up, "Heee Haww!—Heee Haww!"

One armed Anderson sat up and shouted, "GENE (the swamper he had left in Trona), IS THAT YOU?"

I FOUND RUSSELL'S LOST LEDGE

One day, while Carl and I were working in the mine, we cut into a new vein that looked like it might be good silver ore. We were pretty excited and wanted to get an assay of this new formation right away.

Russell was in the habit of making monthly trips to Las Vegas to get supplies, and kick up his heels. We asked him if he could get us an assay report while he was there in "Sin City" and bring us the answer. He said, "Why sure, boys, with my connections it's no problem at all".

Three days went by and finally late in the evening, Russell came in his old GMC one-ton van, up the dirt road and around the bend, rattling along in a cloud of pungent dust. He stopped by our trailer instead of going on around to his clapboard shack.

His cozy camp, with the typical collection of desert artifacts, was just a little further on, in the lee of a small hill. When he stopped short like that we knew he was in a hurry to tell us something. We were sure it must be the news we were waiting for, the news of our new bonanza. When he strolled up the hill from his truck we were happy to see him. That is, we were happy to see him until we asked him for our assay report.

The assay report was not what was on Russell's mind. When we pressed him for it, he could not quite remember what the assayer told him. He said, "Well it might have been one percent silver or it might have been point zero one silver, I did not get a chance to pick up the assay." Of course the difference between the figures he was quoting meant the difference between a fortune and the "poor house," but he was not even bothered by our concern. He went on by us and pulled open the frail battered old screen door to our trailer and went in and sat down on the north bunk. We followed him in and pulled up a couple of chairs. I was quite disappointed and a little angry.

Russell did have quite a dramatic tale to tell, and could he spin a yarn! The story was about a rich widow woman he said he had spent the night with at the El Cortez hotel in the glittering city of Las Vegas. He said she was a redhead and her name was Beatrice Britten. He claimed she was a rich widow from North Platt, Nebraska. He said, "She thought I was her dream come true. Why we spent the whole night together. I really showed her a good time."

Russell helped himself to a bottle of wine that someone had left by the little table near the bunk he was sitting on and went on telling us what a wonderful person he was. I thought that this story of his was going to get even better the next time he told it. I wondered why he would make up a story like that anyway. Was he just trying to brag about the bright lights and the high living that he knew we were missing out on? After rambling on for quite a while, the old man finally lay back on the scruffy bunk and fell asleep. Carl and I were very disgruntled. I told Carl, "Send a kid to town for groceries and what does he come back with, a love story, and at his age!"

The next day Carl and I decided to go to the closest desert town of Shoshone, two hours away across the south end of Death Valley. We would be able to phone the assayer from there to get the real answer about the silver ore. We might have hit a bonanza. We were tired of washing our clothes with a scrub board and we could use the washing machine at the trailer park there.

The assayer did not have any great news for us.

While we were still in Shoshone, I decided to get even with Russell. Suspecting Russell's story, like so many he had told us, was a bit of a fabrication, I decided to call the El Cortez and ask to talk to Beatrice Britten. I figured I would catch Russell in a lie and be able to kid him about it. Seven dollars in telephone change later we were on the way to Las Vegas in our old Dodge pickup truck to meet Beatrice and possibly bring her back to camp with us.

The joke so far was on me. This woman had in fact not only spent the night with Russell, she thought he was a great guy. I almost bit my tongue when she asked me, "Isn't he the nicest person?" My first impulse was to say that he is sort of a desert character in some way comparable to the rattlesnake, however I kept my humor to myself and replied, "Oh yes! A wonderful man."

I wanted to meet this redhead. Through the course of our conversation I found out that she was in fact a retired executive from a woolen mill in North Platte, Nebraska—68-year-old widow with a lot of spunk and a taste for high adventure and she was on vacation in Las Vegas. What an interesting person, I thought.

Suddenly I became fascinated with a new plan. Oh, what the devious mind can do.

I knew that Russell was a typical male chauvinist and though he had a nice fling, having been a bachelor for many years, he had scurried back to his remote desert sanctuary. I wanted to see what would happen if I brought this dynamic lady to the lion's den.

Beatrice decided after talking to me for a long time on the phone that, even though I was a prospector, she would trust me. Later, she told me that the security people at the hotel had told her that a prospector was the last person on earth that she should go off into the desert with. They told her it was not unusual for a woman to meet her end that way, and they painted for her a picture of a remote desert grave. Anyway she decided to go along with my joke and let us take her to camp and surprise Russell.

Carl and I picked Beatrice up at the El Cortez that afternoon. We received a hard look from the hotel employees when we loaded her expensive luggage and fur coat into the old dusty pickup truck. I don't think our worn, un-ironed clothes, Levis and denim shirts, gave anyone any reassurances either.

As we drove south down the Las Vegas strip on our way out of town, Beatrice offered to buy us a drink. Carl said, "I'm a member of Alcoholics Anonymous, don't drink any more, thanks." I said, "If you want, let's have some hot chocolate and pie." I stopped at a small café on the south end of the strip.

It was quite a drive across the desert on the way back to camp and the evening shadows soon closed in, along with the sense of isolation. We were embraced by the walls of "Death Valley" and its absorbing loneliness. Bonded by the remoteness, the three of us packed in the cab of the truck; it wasn't long before we were good friends. Beatrice liked us and she relaxed and we kidded as I drove along in the early moonlight. She confessed that offering to buy us a drink back in Las Vegas had been a test. If we had taken her up on it she would have left us right there. I countered by saying, "You think you were worried? I have just taken you across the state line for immoral purposes". We all laughed and enjoyed the trip down into the great depression and back up into the mountains on the west side, twisting our way up to our Shangri-La type valley in the top of the range.

I will never forget the scene at Russell's that night when we drove into camp. We had warned Beatrice that it was Russell's habit to come out and meet us with his choicest profanity. He did

Panamint Russell in front of his camp. Photo courtesy of Butte Valley Bugle.

not disappoint us. When we drove in Russell came out of his cabin with his typical greeting. "What kept you, you bastards? You sons-a-bitches were only going to God-damn Shoshone," and so-forth. He finally, as he caught his breath, came up to the door of our pickup truck. I said, "Hold on Russ, we brought a friend of yours with us." As he stared into the dark cab, Beatrice said "Hello, Russ". Panamint Russell came awful close to having a heart attack right then. For a while he couldn't say anything. He just sort of stood there, sputtering.

The next morning Carl called me to come look out the window of our trailer. He said, "Ve may have 'done-in' our buddy, Emmett, look." There was Russell scurrying around in the early morning light, wearing an apron and pushing a wheelbarrow trying to pick up and beautify his camp.

With Beatrice there, Russell's Camp did change, and in a hurry. It wasn't long before they had an indoor toilet and shower, also a new bedroom. The first time they went to the big city, Beatrice bought them a new Toyota four-wheel drive, as well as having her town car shipped to Las Vegas and arranging to have it garaged there. Then they went on one adventure after another.

Strange as it may seem I think it is fair to say I found Russell's lost ledge in the lobby of the El Cortez in Las Vegas, Nevada.

MISSING IN ACTION

In 1969 Southern California almost washed away with a rainstorm that set all kinds of records. My son Gerald and I were working at one of our mines high up on the west rim of Death Valley. Since we were out of contact with the rest of the world when the big storm came in, we were unaware that my house in San Bernardino was just about to be washed away. My wife, Ruth, was working with a crew installing a sandbag barrier to save it.

Gerald and I thought the big storm was local. We felt sorry for ourselves and were sure if the folks at home knew what peril we were in they would be worried.

The joke was on us as most of the people in Southern California were busy worrying about their own welfare. Ruth was more than disappointed that I wasn't there to help her!

Even though it was raining while we were working on the west ridge line less than 1/4 mile from the top of Manly Peak, the weather was not too bad in the early morning but by evening you can bet we were down off the mountain. We were headed for Russell's camp ready to hunker down through the deluge. The roof of the trailer at our regular camp leaked and we planned to stay in the van that night.

The noise of the rain had a narcotic effect as the wind rocked the van. Fatigue completed the formula and I was nodding off even though it was still early. If it hadn't been for the storm, we would have been watching the sun set. The sky was gone and we were snug in our sleeping bags. The wind was driving a heavy, horizontal rain against the old GMC, the storm was really lashing out. I was so glad we were out of the wet and the cold. Even in our cramped quarters we felt cozy.

Our van was parked behind Russell's cabin, sheltered by a notch in the side of a hill. Suddenly I was wrenched out of my trance. I was alarmed when I realized that someone was knocking on the van's front door window. Then above the sound of the storm, I heard Beatrice Britten call out, "Emmett, I need some help." "Yes, we will be right with you!" Pulling on our boots and britches, Gerald and I clambered out of the van and rushed Beatrice back into the cabin out of the drenching rain.

In the cabin it was warm, as Beatrice stood there in the dark drying off by the iron parlor stove. The orange light from the cracks in this wonderful old stove gave off enough light to see that this redheaded lady was very upset. The first thing she asked for was help with the Coleman lantern. She had not been able to get it going after the day suddenly darkened.

As I worked on the Coleman lantern, she told us that Russell was missing. She said, "Russell has been gone for three days. He went for supplies and should have been back by now. With this new storm on top of the other rain we have had I am really worried. I'm afraid something has happened to him."

I told her, "Bea, Russell has been making these trips to town in that old white one-ton van of his for a lot of years. Don't worry; he can take care of himself. I feel sure that if he had any trouble he would go to the Grantham Talc Mine for help. He has to go right by it in Warm Springs Canyon on his way up from the floor of Death Valley. Don't worry."

She was not at all convinced. She said, "I will feel a lot better if we drive down there and make sure nothing has happened." I knew that Beatrice had heart trouble and was taking medication, so I was not about to take her out in the night and the storm to look for Russell.

As tired as I was, I understood that this dynamic lady was not about to let up until she got something done. So I told her I would drive down the road and check things out, if she would stay there by the stove and wait for us; the lantern was now glowing brightly. She agreed, and the boy and I set out in our van down the slippery muddy dirt road that went to the north end of Striped Butte Valley to the head of Warm Springs Canyon.

The rain thrashed against our windows and the windshield wipers could hardly help at all, If we had not been familiar with the area we would have run off the road. Even knowing the road did not help in some places. Water was rapidly cutting gouges across our path. We enjoyed the comfort of the cab of the old van with the heater fan purring, outside the wind and the water seemed like a storm-tossed sea.

When we got to the upper end of the Striped Butte Valley, suddenly the road was gone. We had just crested a high spot and as the van tilted down I had to slam on the brakes, we slid to a stop. A roaring stream of water was licking at our front bumper. I instinctively jammed the gearshift into reverse, the rear wheels spun as the van rolled over the rise. Gerald and I looked at each other, I'm sure I looked as surprised as he did. We just sat there for a moment as sheets of rain cut through the twin beams of the van's headlights that were stabbing out into the black void. We got out and climbed up cautiously to the top of the high ground. As we stood there, we could hear the roar of water and we could feel the thumping of the boulders washing down Warm Springs Canyon, spilling into the night. Even in the rain we could smell this river of mud, boulders and brush. This wild stream was where the road to the Grantham Talc Mine should have been, God help Russell if he was in the way.

When we shined our bright 6-volt flashlight down the canyon we could see that it was impossible to go any farther. The torrent had cut us off completely; we could not even walk down the canyon to look for what might have been left of Russell's truck.

On the way back to Russell's camp, Gerald asked me what I was going to tell Beatrice. I said, "Well, I don't know, I guess all we can tell her is that we have to wait till morning and that we will start out again when it is light and the rain lets up. Don't say anything about the washout."

The next morning it was just beginning to be light and it was still raining some when Beatrice woke us up, pounding gently on the side of the van. She said, "Come on, boys, I have got hot cakes ready."

The smell of the coffee and sound of the sizzling pan on the stove made me feel a little better about the day as we sat down at the table in her kitchen that morning.

It was nice to be there in Russell's cabin. Besides the heat from the parlor stove there was a spirit about that shed that gave you a different kind of warmth, a spirit that was there because this place had been a refuge to many others in the past. That feeling was enhanced by this tender, loving woman being there. This was a grand combination.

After breakfast I was reluctant to quit the comfort of the camp but with Beatrice's encouragement we decided to get going even though it was still raining lightly.

I had realized that we could not leave Beatrice there to worry herself sick. It was probably better for her to go with us. The new red Toyota four-wheel drive that Beatrice had bought for Russell was sitting there at the camp. There was a good chance we might be able to use it if we got into trouble trying to negotiate our way through the new gullies. It was seven miles down the washed out canyon to the Grantham mine. I asked Beatrice if she could drive the Toyota and she said, "The salesman in Las Vegas showed me how it works and I think I can drive it, let's go."

When our lonely two-car caravan arrived at the head of Warm Springs Canyon the stream had dissipated and the canyon floor was strewn with a variety of large and small boulders blocking our path. There was no sign of a road. As bad as it looked at least the damp course sand promised good traction. I went ahead, stopping every few feet and getting out of the van and moving boulders wherever I could not drive around them.

The wind was blowing and the sky was still threatening, there was nothing but dark clouds overhead. I worked feverishly and it was still raining and I used a long pry bar to move large stones out of our way. I was constantly plagued by the thought that any minute a new cloudburst might bring a wall of water rushing down on top of us. I knew of several accounts of just such a thing happening. I hoped for some warning that would give me time to run back to the Toyota and drag Beatrice and the boy out and get them up the side of the canyon out of the way. As I worked, I found myself constantly glancing back up the canyon. Beatrice was not having any trouble at all with the Toyota. I was glad she and the boy were at least temporarily warm and dry.

The poncho that I was wearing probably would have been a real asset in calm weather, but here it was no help at all. It kept blowing up in my face or over my head and I finally threw it away in disgust and continued on, drenched by the rain. I was wet but not cold. Working the pry-bar and a come-along, moving the rocks so we could get the vehicles through, was hard work.

Fear pushed me on and time seemed to be suspended. Though it did not seem like it, it took us six hours to get down the canyon. It would ordinarily take less than a half hour. When we finally got down to where the canyon began to widen out into Death Valley we could see the Grantham mine compound, up on a bench on the south side. You can imagine our sigh of relief as we twisted our way out of the streambed, over a ridge, and back onto a section of the road that had survived the washout.

Long view of Warm Springs Camp. Maintenance building in right mid-picture. The talc mine is further along the road in the lower right. Photo by Richard Pope.

When we drove up to one of the metal buildings at the mine, some workmen came out and greeted us. When I asked if "Panamint" Russell was there, one of this hardy desert crew said, "Oh yes, he's been here for two days." Pointing toward the west end of the camp, he said, "Up there drinking whiskey and watching TV with the mine superintendent. You will find him at the silver trailer. Russell left his big van down at the mouth of the canyon the other side of the wash."

I can only imagine Russell's feelings being stuck at the talc mine, not able to get back to his new love and thinking that she was alone at the camp. From what I knew of Russell's life, and I had spent many hours swapping stories with him, I did know that this affair with Beatrice was one of the most exciting things that had ever blessed his life in Death Valley. I was sure they were madly in love.

I knocked at the trailer and called Russell out. From the tears in their eyes you could see how happy Russell and Beatrice were to see each other, but the first thing Russell said to her was, "Where the hell have you been, you old bat? You knew I would need that Toyota." She shouted right back at him as she climbed out of the Toyota, "Why you—you ornery old fart, that's it! I'm on my way back to North Platte. I'm leaving right now with Emmett!"

They kept on shouting as the superintendent and I walked them into the dining hall for some coffee.

He and I sat at another table in the large room and watched as Russell and Beatrice continued their loud discourse. At one point Russell jumped up and said, "You had to know how worried I was about you, for God's sake." He stood up and threw his hat down on the floor, stomping on it to emphasize his words. Beatrice was only encouraged by Russell's demonstration. She said, "Oh for God's sake yourself! I'm sorry I let it rain so hard. I hope you did not strain yourself waiting for me, you old goat!"

The superintendent and I laughed till we had tears in our eyes; he said to me, "Some people say 'I love you' in the strangest way."

❋

Needless to say Beatrice did not leave with me, nor did she go home to North Platte.

Also, needless to say, well, I'll say it anyway; Beatrice Britten was one of the most adventurous women I've ever met. She and Panamint Russell began living it up. What a wonderful time they had. I wasn't around and didn't follow their activities real close after that last episode. But every now and then we would cross trails or I would hear something new about them.

One of the stories that Russell had been telling us over the years was about a meteorite that an Indian in Nevada had seen. This Indian claimed that he knew right where this meteorite had struck the ground. Why he even said this ball of fire had passed right over him! He could show them right where it plowed into the foothills of a mountain. Now that he had Bea to share his dream they set off on the Indian's trail.

Russell told me some of the particulars when he stopped by the camp during their meteor hunt. "You see, Emmett, we are going to find a great deposit of nickel. You know that's what meteors are made of. We can't miss, the old Indian is right there with us most of the time. The progress report he gave at that time went something like this: "We've had some difficulty as the Department of Interior wouldn't let us make a road in to the meteor site. You see, the old Indian had some friends that had a D8 Caterpillar and we've paid them to walk their machine in to where we could dig up the meteorite. The problem was that we couldn't get fuel to the machine. Fortunately the old Indian had a friend who had a string of packhorses. So we rigged up some containers that horses could pack to the Caterpillar. The problem there was that some of the diesel fuel leaked onto the horses and we ended up with a big veterinary bill. Now we have to wait for the horses to heal. But it won't be long before we uncover the richest deposit of nickel in the country."

The next report I got was that they were looking for a new bulldozer operator. It seems that one day their operator climbed up onto his machine and while standing on the tracks he slumped over dead from a heart attack.

When they finally got to digging the old Indian wasn't too sure that this was the right spot. Or maybe the meteorite had gone clear through the mountain. Russell told me they spent $7,000 on the project before the old Indian disappeared.

❋

The next thing I knew Russell and Bea were on their way to visit Mexico. Later Russell told me that they traveled quite a bit and had a wonderful time in Mexico except for the yellow water.

They were burning the candle at both ends, I thought. But what the heck, they were not kids, why not go on an extended honeymoon.

Beatrice never went home to Nebraska. She and Russell spent the last two years of their lives on one trip after another. They may have overdone it, but they sure seemed happy. The last time I saw Russell, he chuckled when I asked him how he was. He said, "Well, Emmett, it's my arm—It's going bad from signing so many checks."

They both died near Los Angeles within a short time of each other after brief illnesses.

Russell's family took care all of his funeral arrangements. I was not able to make good his plans for his internment. He had asked me, "Emmett, when I die I want you to take my ashes to the top of the Striped Butte and bury me there. Then I want you to drink a half-pint of whiskey and then piss on the grave."

I never did understand the symbolism involved in his request, but I did think his choice for a last resting place would have certainly been a grand idea.

THE MANSON FAMILY

Going up Goler Wash in Lucifer with a second load of material to set up the pack station camp was exciting. The Jeep was overloaded. It was also well broken in, I suppose, by service during WWII. It did look like it had been close to the front lines in some conflict. I was having an interesting time negotiating the waterfalls section. Coming around one of the sharp turns it was necessary to pull over to let another old Jeep pass on its way down. The driver was a typical prospector, but a stranger to me.

He stopped and waved, signaling me to stop. He got out and walked across the crunching coarse gravel to my machine. "Mister. I want to warn you that I passed a bunch of "hippies" walking up the canyon. You'll probably overtake them. I don't know what in hell they are doing out here. You better be careful!"

In my backpack was a revolver. After putting it in a handy place between the seats, I started on. In some of the sandier stretches, I noticed footprints and several were barefoot.

Carl had gone on over to Pahrump Valley, Nevada with his pickup truck to get a load of hay. He would be coming up from the Death Valley side. We were to meet at Russell's Camp that evening. I was nervous, hoping Lucifer would make the trip without breaking down. Stopping several times to check and tighten my cargo straps, the hippies were soon forgotten.

After passing Sourdough Springs there is a steep gully to climb out of Goler Wash and head toward Mengel Pass. When we, Lucifer and I, were successfully up on the higher ground I stopped and got out and stretched and gave thanks to God Almighty. Walking around the machine I didn't see any more footprints. Remembering the hippies, I guessed they must have turned off or something, somewhere back in the wash.

I always stopped halfway through, at the cairn that marked the grave of Carl Mengel. A lonely pile of rocks, cone-shaped, six feet high with a steel wagon tire wrapped around the pile near the base. Billy Meyers had buried his friend's ashes here, marking the spot with a carved mill stone from an old arrastré. Carl

Carl Mengle's grave in Mengle Pass—the southern gateway to Striped Butte Valley. Photo by Ron McKinley.

Mengel had been a real prospector. He spent over thirty years in this part of the Valley. He had lost part of one leg early on in a mine accident, but it never slowed him down. I've talked with men who prospected with him, and they told me he could go places they couldn't. As it turned out he even had a secret camp on top of Manly Peak. Hat in hand, I gave a silent prayer. Little did I know how close our paths were going to be.

Carl Ruona got in just before dark. He was up at first light as usual. Carl may have had an aversion to using a shovel, but he didn't mind leaning into any other task. We had the corral and hitching post ready in one day. The base camp we set up for the pack train was right next to Russell's cabin.

Two weeks after we got the pack animals and were packing ore down from the Lost Mormon mine, we had some unexpected visitors. It was late in the afternoon after we had unpacked and corralled the animals when we noticed that seven people were walking up the dirt road toward our little trailer. The shadows were long and we were just starting dinner. We were of course surprised to see that many people coming out of the dusk. There were four men and three women. They, as it turned out, were part of the group that had been coming up Goler Wash when I came in with the last load of supplies. They were some of the "hippies" the prospector had warned me about.

Their spokesperson was wearing a western shirt and blue jeans and a cowboy-style felt hat. He was not a big man and his voice was soft. The rest seemed younger than he did. "We've been hiking all day. Come around that way," he gestured and waved toward Anvil Wash. "Where did you start from?" I asked, still startled. "We are at that camp near the Myers'."

I was more amazed by his answer. If I understood him right, they were at the Barker mill site and they had walked several miles that day through some very rugged landscape.

It was obvious then that was why there weren't any tracks after Sourdough Springs, they had turned off toward the Barker's and the Myers' camps there.

The place he said they were at belonged to the Barker family, who also leased the Indian Ranch north of the ghost town of Ballarat. When they told me where they were staying, I agreed to give them an introduction to Mrs. Barker and said, "I know she will be glad for you to use the camp, if you'll fix it up a bit."

"We heard that you have a gold mine up here and we would like to work for you guys. I am Charles Manson and my friend here is Charles Watson." Watson stepped forward and put out his hand. He was taller, good looking, and seemed very personable. As we talked he told me he was from Texas. Looking around our camp he could see that we were using pack animals. "I used to work at a dude-ranch. I can help with your pack train."

There was no way we wanted to take strangers up to our mine.

"We'll put on some extra grub. You must be hungry. It's a long walk up from the Barker claim. As far as work at the mine, no, it's a small operation barely big enough for Carl and me."

Dinner over we talked some more and I said, "You want some work to do? We can give you a burro and pack saddle and there may be something you can work down near your camp."

Carl had taken a picture of me talking to them. In the picture I looked like a guru lecturing to this bunch of hippies. The group had gathered around me in a semi-circle and there I was gesturing, pointing with my right hand like a lecturer. *Life Magazine* ended up with this picture. Fortunately for me they did not publish it as someone might have thought I was part of their infamous group. [Note: Subsequent investigation and personal interviews have given the author information about at least five people that were murdered by the family in the area covered by this book. Even now we meet Manson followers camping in these badlands.]

Charlie Manson left and Carl Ruona right. Photo taken in 1968 at Barker Ranch by Chuck Hatch, an ore buyer.

The magazine did use a picture of Carl standing with Charles Manson by a Greenbrier Van at the Barker claim (now referred to as the Manson Camp). That picture came from a mining engineer friend of ours, Chuck Hatch, who was visiting us to pick up some high-grade ore from our mine. He was with us when we stopped by their camp then. About a year later when that issue of the magazine hit the stands, Carl heard from friends as far away as Florida wanting to know what his connection with Charles Manson was—Carl was quite humiliated by that picture.

Other than Russell's friends and Stella Anderson at Greater View Springs these new folks were our closest neighbors.

We didn't see these new neighbors again for a while, however we were to have a lot more to do with them in the future.

MANSON'S HOBBIT CANYON MINE

When Mrs. Barker gave her permission to Charlie Manson and his followers to use the mill site camp in upper Goler Wash they gave her one of the *Beach Boy's* million copy gold records. It wasn't too long after that before members of the Manson family came by and asked Carl and me to come down and visit them.

Author at the Hobbit Canyon Caves. Photo by the author.

"We have discovered some gold ore. Maybe. We would like to see what you think of it."

It was a clear mild morning when we arrived at the little adobe-style building with its wrap-around porch. We had talked with some of the boys before, explaining how they could file claim papers and discussed prospecting and mining a bit with them. But now they wanted us to go see their gold prospect. They had some pieces of ore that did look like it had gold in it.

As they talked with us something didn't seem right. First of all, they were disappointed when Carl and I weren't too interested in their find. I had a strange feeling that they expected we would be excited and greedy enough to be vulnerable, that if we would covet their claim they would have an advantage. In the midst of this I also had a stray thought, "Maybe one or the other of us has seen too many movies." As it turned out, my apprehension was probably well founded. We, as it turned out, were dealing with a master deceiver. (And I also want to remind you that Carl and I had a well-stocked camp and lots of equipment, two vehicles and a string of pack animals. We were all alone and if anything happened to us no one would miss us for a month or two.)

"I've told you guys how to file claim papers. If you think you have something get it recorded," I told them.

They insisted they wanted to show us where they had found their samples. Carl decided I could go with the boys, and he'd stay with Charlie and the girls.

Four of the men went with Charles (Tex) Watson and me. We drove down a short ways to Sourdough Springs and then just around the end of a big ridge we parked. There was a narrow wash leading to the southeast and it was not wide enough to drive into. We started hiking up the slope on the south side of the wash. I had my backpack on and somehow the fact that my revolver was in it gave me more confidence. As we were hiking, the younger men started telling me about the geological formation that we would come to at the head of the wash. They, as it turned out, were fascinated by this mudstone formation because of its "magic."

While climbing on this side hill above the wash we crossed a layer-like formation; spilling down the slope from this strata were roundish, knobby chocolate brown rocks, some large and some small. "Stop here for a minute," I called. "Here is a field of geodes, volcanic rock bubbles. Sometimes there will be cavities inside these rocks lined with crystals." Soon we found some that were broken open by natural erosion and they were either lined with crystals or filled with colorful agate. It was quite a surprise for me to find these geodes. I had never run across any mention of them from any of the locals, nor had there been anything in any mineral reports we had seen.

"Tex, we'll pay you to pack some of these out of here for us, if you will. Here is work you guys can do close to your camp.

"Now let's see where you found the gold ore."

They stepped aside into a group and had a short conference. "I think it's up this way," one of them said, pointing on up toward the large mud-stone formation that boldly jutted over the top of the ridge ahead of us, like a mountain of cake dough. All of a sudden the location of their gold mine-to-be had become vague. We crossed over to the north side of the wash where it was not quite as steep and continued climbing. I was careful to stay apart

Hobbit Canyon caves where "the imaginary little people lived. Also the Manson Family's "magic spot". Photo by author.

and slightly above. When we stopped at the crest, one of them, I believe it was Paul Watkins, explained to me that they thought the mudstone formation that we were now facing, was very special. "See those small caves and cavities. See inside some of them, there are little stone tables, and there are miniature chairs, too. These are Hobbit houses. A place for the spirits."

"Come on! Let's go over to that side."

The formation was picturesque, but I didn't know anything about their little people.

"No. I have got to get back, have to meet some people in Trona," I lied. "Where's that outcrop of quartz we came up to see?"

"Well its around here somewhere," someone said from almost behind me. I walked farther uphill.

Tex came uphill too. And just as he did, all of a sudden, close by, there was the sound of an engine. As we looked in that direction, a small plane popped over the ridge to the west of us. It was real low skimming the hillside. Tex looked back and forth between the plane and me hurriedly. I dropped off my pack and in the same smooth motion I pulled out of one of the side pockets a stainless steel signal mirror. Tex said, "What are you doing?" as I began reflecting a beam of sunlight at the plane.

"That's a friend of mine! I'm letting him know where I am," I lied again.

And, as if on cue, whoever it was in the plane dipped the wings in answer to my signal.

I guessed there was some kind of magic there after all—on my side anyway.

We headed back after that and there was no more talk that day about the gold. I wondered about Carl as we had been gone for quite awhile.

When we got back to Barker's place, Carl and Charlie came out laughing and talking. I guessed they had got along all right while I was gone. But the old Finlander hadn't been brainwashed into their commune.

Finding the geodes worked out. The next time I came by their camp there was a large pile of geodes on the porch. They had packed out over a half of a ton of them for me. I traded them a truckload of food for a truckload of semiprecious specimens. I recently rediscovered that geode area, but they must have pretty much scoured off all the ones that were exposed.

About the gold mine: when the authorities finally raided their camp and arrested everyone that was there, one of the things they found there was a pile of good gold ore stacked up behind one of the buildings.

When I, after all these years, went back and climbed up on the hills to the south, I looked down on this forlorn little claim site that had been the desert refuge for the *family*—this *family* that became so famous, having been involved in several horrendous murders. A flood of emotions swept through my mind. I did not want to believe—it was terribly sad. All the horrible things they did seemed so incongruous with the peace and serenity that embraces this oasis. Oh, the things that need not have happened!

From my high vantage place, when I turned and looked to the south, below me I could see the pack trail that they had built to their gold mine. As I understand it the members that split off from Mason and his followers and eventually escaped from them during the last days of the *family*, were the ones that became interested in prospecting and mining. They were too busy to be out trying to bring about Armageddon. These survivors were among the last of the Death Valley Prospectors.

Now of course most people know that Charles, Tex, and many of his associates were caught and convicted of several murders. Vincent Bugliosi writes about some of their victims in his book "*Helter Skelter*." [Note: I was questioned by the prosecution and they decided I would be a poor witness for them as I could not honestly say that I had seen anything that would have helped them. By contrast, they told me a great deal about the family's activities in the valley that I hadn't been aware of. They interviewed me by telephone once and again in person at Ballarat ghost town. The defense never contacted me.]

AN EVENING AT
MANSON'S CAMP

The main building at the Barker mill site wasn't large, only two and a half rooms. There was a small closet in the corner of the main room that had an old pull-chain tank toilet and a one-door cabinet with washbasin built into the top of it. The architect did not waste any space (Charles Manson was later arrested when an officer, who was relieving himself in this facility, noticed a flock of Charles' long hair sticking out of the closed cabinet door). Basically the building consisted of a kitchen that opened into the living room with a little bedroom off to the side. There was a

Author standing on the porch of the Barker Camp (Manson Camp) in Goler Wash. Photo by Ron McKinley.

porch that swung around the front of the adobe type structure. A medium sized cottonwood tree set off the scene; gracefully standing guard in the front yard that was designated by a feeble wire fence. Around to the west side there was a storage shed. (I had helped "Ballarat Bob" to fix up this shed for a separate sleeping space when he was the former tenant.) Out back, to the north, was a rectangular stone and cement water tank almost four feet high that was sometimes used as a swimming pool.

The Barkers built their camp in a small canyon that drains into the head of Goler Wash. The Myers Family had a well-developed camp a short distance northeast. Billy Myers, the patriarch of his family, had been a successful prospector in these parts

Outside view of the main building at the Barker Camp (Manson Camp). Photo by Ron McKinley.

for many years and there could be a book or two written about him. He built up his camp as a comfortable family retreat. Years before any of this happened I often saw his daughters or grandchildren in Goler Wash on their way in or out of their place. I only met him a couple of times and I am sorry that I did not find the time to know him better. I admired him and what he had accomplished while mining and road building in Death Valley. Besides mining and prospecting, he was a schoolteacher as well. I believe he taught in San Bernardino, California. Though Billy had handled explosives all of his life, astonishingly he died as the result of a dynamite explosion a few years before the Manson family came along. I once sat and talked with his widow for a long time one afternoon at their lovely cabin that was nestled in amongst several shade trees. Her granddaughter "Cappy" was very close to her grandfather and when Billy died she was devastated. Cappy told me, when I met her at the Manson camp, that her parents were having a lot of trouble at the time of Billy's death and that was when she had run away to Haight-Ashbury (San Francisco's hippie district at that time). She was fourteen then.

When I met her she was a tall, beautiful, seventeen-year-old brunette. It was Cappy who directed the Manson clan to the camp and they had moved in next door to her family's sanctuary.

Most of the Panamint Mountains are bold, drab and rocky. These camps however were hidden in a natural garden; this stretch of the canyon is an oasis, there is quite a bit of water and plants along the north bank, and right at Sourdough Springs, the entrance to this green land, it is almost blocked by a stand of cottonwoods that straddle a delicate year-round stream.

This is a peaceful place, but when cloudbursts come, about once every nine years, it can turn into a small Niagara. One year a storm almost washed the Myers Camp down into Goler Wash.

The evening that I am talking about, when Carl and I stopped by the Manson Camp, it was a bit chilly and the cast iron camp stove was glowing. It was located just out of the kitchen, into the living room space. Carl and Charley were settled down in comfortable chairs, one on either side of the stove, talking. I was just a few feet away at the kitchen table that was really a picnic table that had found its way into this mountain hideaway. There were four or five women doing different things around the kitchen range across the room. I was talking to a couple of girls at the table. The ladies were dressed in a variety of outfits, some denoting the peace symbol theme of that time, headband and so forth.

Our hostesses had put a big platter filled with hot syrup in the middle of the table. The cooks were shuttling from the range to the table bringing us stacks of steaming hotcakes. We were rolling the hotcakes up like tortillas and dipping them in the syrup. It was a communal platter of syrup.

Carl, in his Finland accent was saying, "You hippies," and so forth, when Charles Manson took exception to the term "Hippies." "We are not Hippies. That is why we left Haight-Ashbury. We came out here to get away from the troubles of the world."

"Vel, Charlie, you're a damn fool. Don't you know that you don't get away from the trouble nowhere—you yust trade one set of troubles for another. Now here you are, out of coffee and tobacco and so forth, ya, you yust trade one trouble for another anywhere in da world."

Charlie sputtered at Carl's very apt homespun logic.

I have had more than one opportunity to look back, remembering times like this, and now that I am a lot older I appreciate how smart Carl Ruona was. He gave some great advice, but as usual, here it was wasted. I don't for a minute think that Charlie ever realized that it was his habit to always make the worst trade possible when it came to trouble.

As their conversation went on Charlie changed the subject, "Here is what it says in the *Book of Revelations*, and he quoted

Author in the kitchen of the Barker Camp (Manson Camp). Note the logbook on the table where visitors are expected to sign in. Photo by Ron McKinley.

verse after verse. Right then he was a self-styled evangelist. And from the photo that *Life Magazine* published of Carl and Charlie standing together you will see that he dressed like a cowboy and was much different then. Now he is a less than remarkable man who babbles on, trying to look like a fiend from hell. Then we didn't recognize him as a social reformer or guru; he was not a big man and he was soft spoken. But of course, Carl and I were not runaway girls or wayward boys looking for someone to follow. We were just gold hungry prospectors. As we found out later, Charlie would use the girls and their physical charms as sort of a magic elixir (as well as a variety of chemicals) to cloud the brains of men in order to persuade them to follow him. Some of the girls were quite attractive looking, however Carl and I were immune. We were only after gold, thank God!

We did not see this group as part of our prospector circle, even though at that time they were often, like I said, our closest neighbors, only seven miles away.

Panamint Russell did not think much of the folks staying at the Barker camp; he had met them when they stopped by his place. He said, "Them hickeys ain't no damn good, Emmett." Well I was young and knew all the answers then, and besides that, I loved to argue with Russell, " Oh! Come on Russ, they're just young people finding their way in these special times. Whereas you are just a stubborn ornery old man, that's what's a matter with you!" Little could I have imagined that Manson and some of his followers would, within a short time, become famous world-over for having committed gruesome and senseless mass murders as well as other deleterious crimes.

If it is possible for a ghost to turn over in his grave, I guess it is Russell, who had the last laugh and is probably still chuckling. I will still claim I was right, to a degree. There were many young men and women who wandered, or were enticed, into the Barker camp or the Spahn Ranch in San Fernando Valley (the movie ranch that became their launch pad for crime) and then decided to get the hell out of that mess in a hurry.

Not long ago Bill Mann and I stopped to see the Barker camp again and as I walked through the empty building I felt tears well up in my eyes as I remember the horror and pain that came from here, and yet I still feel sadness and compassion for the perpetrators. I had seen them when they were better people and before they had twisted all the knobs off their brains with stupid chemicals. I tell youngsters sometimes now, "Don't be too damn smug, unless <u>you</u> decide to make the <u>right</u> choices, God help you too." I have been condemned for saying anything kind concerning this episode, but some of the condemners scare me worse than Charlie did. I think I can see behind their super sanctimonious mask, an ugly, black shrouded character, viciously moaning, "Hate, hate."

❋

Before I close on that evening, I do remember a scene that will bring some of the social dilemma in their group to light. In order to explain, I first have to share with you what happened one morning when Carl and I were staying at the stone cabin at Anvil Springs. We were awakened by the bellowing and snorting of a wild herd of burros that had moved in around the spring during the night. The sun was already warming Striped Butte Valley and

Author in the living room, pointing to the bedroom, of the Barker Camp (Manson Camp). Photo by Ron McKinley.

the butte was bold in the morning light, its colors so vivid. Carl was looking out one of the other windows and he laughed and motioned me over to see. There was a gray battered jack burro who looked like he had more than enough; his head was down and his ears were drooping sadly. But the ruckus was coming from two jennies who were backing up to him, kicking and demanding him to get to work.

Now back to the warm little cabin at the Barker Ranch that night. When we were getting up to leave, we noticed two young men standing in the living room and they said, "These nights are getting real cold." There was a demure voice that called out from the dark bedroom, "You won't be cold if you come in here with us like we told you." The men looked at each other and I thought I saw a glimmer of fear in their eyes and they did look a bit battered. They silently headed for the outside door. Carl and I laughed later when we compared these young men to the poor jack burro and his anguish.

Also, before it is forgotten, let's talk about the "washing machine." One day, later, when I happened to stop by the Barker camp on the way to town I found one of the women there, who was dressed in a pink, frilly outfit, swinging in an old weathered tire that was hanging by a faded rope from the front yard cottonwood tree. The picture reminded me of a scene from the movie, *Gods Little Acre.* I believe the character was *Darling Jill.* "Hi, Emmett, I am so glad to see you." She unwound herself from her pendulum, coming to the Jeep, she beckoned me to get out and follow her. "Come see our new "washing machine." I did not believe that they had a generator and I wondered what kind of a machine she was talking about. As we came around the side of the main building, I could hear a great deal of laughter.

There in the shallow water tank were four girls. Two brunettes, a redhead, and a blond, quite naked, not models cloned for *Playboy* but real people, different sizes and shapes, frolicking as if they were preparing for a Roman festival. They were having a wonderful time treading their clothes as if they were stomping grapes. It was without a doubt the fanciest washing machine in Death Valley!

Barker Camp swimming pool, a.k.a. the Manson Washing Machine, is in a sad state of repair now. Photo by Ron McKinley.

PETER B. KYNE'S SECRET CAMP

This camp is hidden in a majestic natural fortress. It is still an adventure to get to it today. I tried to land a helicopter there but the mountains were too rugged for us to set down anywhere nearby. Sandy Hunt and I were in this camp once. It was really an extraordinary experience.

In the 1920s and 30s, Peter B. Kyne wrote several best selling books: *Never the Twain Shall Meet, The Enchanted Hill, The Parson of the Panamints,* to name a few. His western stories were great and some were made into movies. One of my favorites was, *The Three Godfathers*, starring John Wayne and Ward

Sketch of Peter B. Kyne.

Bond. He also wrote serialized stories for the *Saturday Evening Post* magazine.

I heard stories about this camp from Russell years before we got to see it. When he first started talking to us about this place. I was not interested in chasing around the hills looking for some dumb thing that he thought was important. Like everything he talked about, there was a weird mystery that went with it. At that time I had no idea who Peter B. Kyne was. For a long time, I thought he was telling us about some guy named called "Peter be kind".

✳

Another Panamint Russell Story.

Several years before, in the 1950s, during the Uranium Fever that came with nuclear power, there was a great deal of prospecting for radioactive minerals. There was a multitude of people dreaming of getting rich fast. There was a period when lots of men and women were out in the hills with "Geiger counters." Supposedly, during that time, Russell and a friend of his happened to have been visiting with a woman who was related in some way to Peter B. Kyne's widow. She lived in downtown Los Angeles.

During their visit they noticed a large black rock that she was using for a doorstop. When Russell examined the rock, he discovered that it was very heavy and yet it did not look like metal. In fact, it did not resemble any mineral they were familiar with.

They did not have a Geiger counter or any instrument to detect radiation, so they decided to jury-rig a test to see if this might be uranium ore. They took a new roll of film and set it a short distance from the rock. Then they hung a metal key on a string between the film and the mystery rock. After what they thought was a sufficient amount of time, they pulled the film away.

They hurried to find a photo shop that could develop the film for them right away. When they got the exposed roll back, there was a row of images of the key, over and over, one key for each layer of film on the packaged roll. Strong radiation from the rock had penetrated clear though the whole package of film!

This set off a wild adventure. Russell and his associates were going to find where this rich piece of rock, this black beauty of uranium ore, had come from. Well would you believe it, as it turned out it came from the badlands just a few miles from Russell's Death Valley prospecting cabin.

It seems that when they asked where the rock came from, they were told that Peter B. Kyne had found it while taking a walk above his writing hideaway, located in the mountains that rimmed the west side of Death Valley, the Panamint Mountains.

The story was, that when it was the right time of year, Peter would slip away out of Ballarat into the Panamint Mountains. He went with a packer he hired to help him outfit his stay there. They were supposed to have gone up into the Panamints via Redlands Canyon. This was the same canyon some of the ill-fated Death Valley Forty-Niners had used to escape from their deadly entrapment.

Redlands Canyon, if you travel all the way to the top, leads into Shangri-La—Butte Valley, where Russell's cabin was nestled in a cluster of trees and brush at the top of a small branch of a canyon.

Once Peter and his companion made their way part way up out of Panamint Valley into Redlands Canyon (a couple of miles) they ordinarily stopped at a base camp. This rest stop was where a side canyon came in; it was hidden in the floor of the steep canyon somehow. There was supposed to be a typical fireplace made out of natural rocks with an iron bar for hanging the coffee pot. That fireplace was the kick-off spot for the track that led to the secret camp. The camp was supposed to be on the north side of the canyon. The trail was supposed to go up the other side, the steep, almost vertical, south wall of Redlands Canyon. [I could imagine Peter and his companion waiting there at this first camp until they were sure no one would follow them. I would suppose when the coast was clear, they would spirit their outfit across the wash and up the trail to their hideout, out of sight.]

The final camp, at the top of this steep trail, as Russell told it, was cut out of the solid granite ridge, a small shelter with a wooden frame covered with canvas.

Russell told me that he and his friends had found the camp after much difficulty and that they marked the spot by fashioning a large cross out of some of the old timber that had been packed in there. He said, "We propped the cross up so it projected up from a notch that had been cut in the ridge for the shelter. We fixed it upright with bailing wire that we found there."

He explained, "The idea was that we would be able to line up on the camp from the main ridge of the western fork of the mother mountain." They felt this would lead them in from the top and they could cover the area where they thought Peter had found the heavy rock.

The treasure hunters were in a big hurry and the idea of climbing around in that rough terrain was not what they were interested in. They rented an airplane and flew around trying to find a shiny black ledge where the mystery rock might have come from.

He said, "The problem was that we couldn't see the cross from the main part of the mountain." They flew back and forth over the camp and dropped cans of paint in order to mark the spot better. Still, they did not find the origin of the rock. In the end, after much time and confusion, they deferred the search.

❋

Sometimes when we were sitting around talking in Russell's kitchen shack (more mining and secret adventures happened around the little table than you could imagine), Russell would tell me that I needed to go down Redlands Canyon and see this place. He would say, "You just go down there. You find the spot in the canyon floor, the fireplace, then, go to the other side of the canyon and you will find the trail, follow it to the camp. That's all."

Finally, after he kept after me time and time again one Sunday while I was taking it easy, I went down Redlands Canyon looking for this secret place. The sandy wash gets narrower and steeper as you sink toward Panamint Valley—it's a good place to get a vehicle stuck. I did not find anything.

After looking for it a couple of times and not finding any trace of the base camp or any trail, I asked Russell to go down with me and show me where it was. "I can't go right now, people are coming up from L.A. to visit me," or some other excuse. He would say, "I can't leave camp, just find the fireplace." I told him, "Hey! I've looked and looked, no rod or anything." He said, "Well, that's because we carried off all the junk from there and the dishes and things from the high camp too. Just look for the place where the smoke blackened the rock wall above the camp fire, that's all!"

He kept after me to go see Peter B. Kyne's camp, but each time I wanted him to go with me, it was the same kind of excuse.

Sandy Hunt was a friend of Russell's who visited him often. Sandy loved to prowl around that part of Death Valley, like I did. He was an engineer for the Navy Department and he worked at their high security facility, China Lake Naval Air Station. China Lake is where the U.S. Navy tests some of their high-tech equipment. It's a dry lake in the desert not far west of Death Valley.

Russell had also tried to persuade Sandy to find Peter B. Kyne's camp but he had the same bad luck that I had. He didn't find the camp and couldn't get Russell to show him where it was.

I had met Sandy several times at Russell's cabin and we enjoyed talking about the mysteries of this forbidden country. Sandy was a tall, intelligent adventurer. We visited each other's homes and our wives were good friends. We both loved the desert, the folklore, and the adventure in this part of the Great Mojave Desert.

Early one Sunday morning when Sandy and I were eating breakfast at Russell's we started talking about Russell's Peter B. Kyne story. "While Carl's in town, why don't you and I go down Redlands Canyon, Sandy, and see if we can find that camp. We won't even tell Russ we are going." "O.K.!" Sandy said, "Sure, let's go."

It was still early when we got into the general area where the camp was supposed to be. We were only about six miles from

Russell's camp. The shadows were still in control of the canyon, but the morning sun was beginning to scour the higher stone-walls of the mountain high above us.

Sandy was driving his International Scout 4-wheel drive. About halfway down the canyon, he stopped in the middle of the wash. The floor of the canyon was less than a hundred feet across and was covered with a variety of multi-colored stone fragments that had been left by scouring thunderstorms. As we got out and stretched, there was just the crunching sound of our boots on the loose stone debris. The sound was amplified by nearly vertical slabs of rock on either side of us. The noise sounded foreign and ghostly in this setting.

As I raised my arms toward the sky, I filled my lungs with the refreshing, cool air. Air scented by the sagebrush that grew in clumps and clusters here and there, clinging desperately wherever it could root and hang on. This canyon, a thousand-foot deep crack, was a dynamic channel for wind and water when the Storm Gods came this way. Sandy and I were both looking up. Sandy said, "Look up there! See where the sunlight has just reached the south side. There! Way up, don't you see that outcrop? It doesn't look natural, does it?"

I said, "Hey! You're right. Where are your binoculars?"

With the help of the glasses, the spot he was talking about did look a bit like a man-made rock wall. It was several hundred feet up the steep slope, too far to be sure. The idea though was very exciting. We were no longer laughing at Panamint Russell.

I said, "Let's climb up toward that outcrop, maybe we can find the trail." Sandy said, "Well, Emmett, that may not be anything. It's a long way up there, isn't it?"

"I am going to go up a ways and see what I can find," I told him.

"My ankles are weak, Emmett, I think I'll wait here at the Scout, O.K."?

I wasn't forty feet up the slope when I crossed the trail, a real nice trail, one like the old Mormons used to make in this part of the country. I was surprised and thrilled and I shouted, "Here it is! This is a neat trail and it's headed toward that area where we saw that rockwork."

Now if this was the right area, the base camp was supposed to have been near where Sandy had stopped the Scout. There was a large drainage that came into the wash at right angles from the north. Sandy said, "Emmett, I am going to look and see if I can find their base."

Sandy had to shout, because I was already flying up the trail. As I looked back, I could see why it was easy to miss finding this route. It did not meet the wash right opposite where the Scout was parked, but tapered at an angle, down into the wash two hundred feet farther up the canyon. Many years of cloudbursts and rock-fall, or someone who wanted to hide it, had masked the beginning of the trail. Was this really the way to Peter B. Kyne's hideout?

Our excitement grew as Sandy, who had been prowling around in the brush, where a large drainage came in from the north, shouted to me, "I have found the base camp, right here!" He was waving his arms in the air. As it turned out there was some camp gear under the brush and a metal fixture to hang a coffee pot on; the camp gear Russell had said he had removed.

Up, up I went. The trail switched back and forth and the rockwork was beautiful—whoever did this was a master trail builder—it seemed as if I was gliding. The virgin rocks around me were covered with a bacterial patina, the desert varnish that cried out, "I've been here exposed to the elements for millions of years and this is my country and you are out of place, mister." There were no smooth edges. They were sharp and bold, not a fit place for the timid. Everything was dark brown or black—still all in the shadows.

Suddenly I was there. In the middle of this primordial world there was a man-made refuge. By this fact alone, it was certainly a magic place.

I was almost a thousand feet above the floor of the wash standing in the bright sunlight. Looking almost straight down on the small Scout and the smaller human figure nearby, my cry of acclaim violated the air, echoing from wall to wall. Sandy later swore that I had teleported myself up there, first shouting to him

I had found the trail, and then the next time he looked up, I was at the camp.

The view from the camp was awesome, not only because my lofty purchase was enhanced by the deep canyon below me, but also to the west I could see Panamint Valley and its dry lake beds. My view of the valley was bracketed by the still, dark walls of Redlands Canyon, like the curtains on each side of a grand theater proscenium. The newborn sun was already highlighting the stark-white swirls of the salt beds. A crystal sea trapped by the brown brush-covered shoreline with the multi-colored slate mountains farther on was a fitting backdrop for this stage.

This refuge had been someone's Valhalla. I did not feel alone there. As I stood looking around I realized that for me the shroud of mystery had only grown a little thinner. There were several puzzling things that did not match the story Russell had told us.

The camp was on a level platform about 20 feet long and 12 feet wide. The platform had been created by filling in the area between the ridgeline and a 15-foot-high rock wall that dammed off a crook in the ridge. The same mason that built the trail must have built the wall—the mortarless wall was ingenious.

There was no granite notch. There had been a tent with a wooden frame, big enough for two people to sleep in. The tent was midway on the platform and it butted up against the ridge behind it, forming a wall four feet high. The canvas had tattered and blown away a long time ago and the wooden frame had collapsed. The rock wall at the back of the tent had been lined with shelves that were now buried by erosion.

There were bottles and silverware in the shelf area. In fact, a variety of miscellaneous items were scattered about the platform.

There was a large wooden cross, like Russell had described, but it was not sticking out of the roof of the shelter. The cross had been erected on the ridge above the tent, fastened in place with guy lines made of bailing wire. It now lay prone like a dead soldier, all anchors had failed.

I suddenly felt like I had been had; I would not have been surprised if someone had cried out, "Gotcha!" I thought to myself that if Russell had ever been at this place he would not have described it the way he did. I felt a bit foolish, but now I understood why he would not show me where it was. He either had never been there or he had not been able to find it again himself.

I thought about Peter B. Kyne and the story about him walking around behind his camp. Well, there was no place to walk. I climbed back off the platform to where the trail had brought me to the ridge. The trail stopped there, and above it the mountain was almost vertical. Then something made me take a closer look.

The patina that covered the face of the slope was missing. Some of the rocks had been disturbed. The lighter colored talus looked like a path someone had tried to hide, so I followed my notion. This path did not go up the mountain—it paralleled the camp. In less than a hundred feet, I came to a cleft where there had been a makeshift "blacksmith" shop. On a hard flat boulder there were still some miner's tools. This stone anvil had served as a forge. Nearby, was the skeleton of a large bellows with black chunks of charcoal scattered about.

This had to have been a mine camp as well as a writer's hideout. Was there a secret mine somewhere around there? From the blacksmith's shop there was an obvious trail and it continued to wind along the slope staying level with the camp.

In just a short distance there was a large outcrop of blue quartz jutting out from the slope. Nestled under the blue outcropping there was the head-frame of a tunnel. There was, in fact, a secret mine! It was a gold mine—I could tell from the geology!

Needless to say, I was very excited. Did Russell know about the mine? I was no longer relaying any information down to Sandy. I was in a private world all my own, me and the ghost of Peter B Kyne. I didn't know if I was going to share this discovery with anyone.

As I hurriedly tried to find a book of matches, the thought came to me that while Peter B. Kyne worked at the camp the packer was busy here at the mine. One thing for sure, they would not have been disturbed by someone dropping in, not unless they came by "Eagle Express."

When I was ready to explore the mine, I noticed there was a name scrawled in bold letters on the lintel of the head frame above the tunnel. The name was "Ben Williams." For me this pulled back the veil a little further. Ben had been dead for many years. He was one of the nicest people you ever wanted to meet. I had gotten to know Ben when I first started to prowl around Butte Valley. I met him before I ever knew Russell. He used to be the caretaker at Russ's Camp before Russell had retired and come out to Death Valley to stay. I loved Ben; he was one of those people that everyone liked; he was just the opposite of Russell as he always told the truth and he was very generous.

Aerial view of Peter B. Kyne's secret camp and gold mine. Mine is at the left part of the circle and camp on the right side. Photo by author.

Russell used to get upset with Ben. He did not like the way Ben would leave the cabin door unlocked when he was out prospecting or showing some visitors around. He did not like it when Ben would leave a note on the table that asked any visitors to leave a message on the calendar pad. Russell always wanted things locked up. He and Ben used to argue often, like the odd couple, but Ben was the only one that Russell could get to stay way out here a long way from the city lights. Russell could afford Ben, and Ben liked it living at the top of the mountains.

Ben had told me, "I can't stay down in Trona (a desert town near China Lake). There is a widow woman down there that worries me to death; she wants to cook and care for me. Her home cooking would finish this old man off."

Anyway, I was beginning to get the picture now. Ben had been up here and he probably had told Russ some things about the camp. Ben had probably done all the legwork, and now that Ben was gone, it was my guess that Russell had not been able to locate the place.

This wasn't the first time Russell had made a sucker out of me, but this time I had more pieces of the puzzle than he did.

By match light I could see that the miner had been going after pocket ore, little bits of gold trapped in vugs (cavities), where pockets of sulfides that contained gold weathered away, leaving behind the base metal. I could not see any rich ore showing but by the flickering light I could see he had dug a tunnel in two directions. There was an intersection about 15 feet in from the portal.

When I got back down to the 4-wheel drive, Sandy was waiting for my report. I told him there was more to the story than Russell had told us. As I went on explaining what was up there, Sandy got excited, so excited that he forgot all about his weak ankles and said, "Emmett, let's go, show me the way. I've got to see this." So we were back up at Mr. Kyne's hideout and a good part of the day had slipped away. The sun was high overhead.

With a flashlight we looked around. The mine looked more interesting. We took vein samples at the mine that later showed about a half an ounce of gold per ton. We didn't dig around, though. At the forge we took some tools; I have a miner's spoon from there, a metal rod fashioned so it can be used to clean out drill holes to make room for explosives. There were silverware and bottles at the camp; I have an old beer bottle that was made in a wooden mold. It has a prominent place in my office. Sandy ended up with a large purple whiskey bottle he was going to make into a vase.

We went on around the wall of the canyon beyond the mine and up the slope a long way, but we did not find any of the black, heavy rock that had started Russell's treasure hunt. However, higher up near the top, too high up, there was an area where there were dark bands of bedrock exposed.

It was late afternoon, almost evening when we got back to Russell's place. The shadows were long on the east side of the mountain. Sandy had to leave and Russell and I were there alone in the small kitchen section of the shack. Russ was putting some beans on the stove.

I told Russell, "Oh yes, Russ, we went down to Peter B. Kyne's camp today."

"How did you find it?" The high pitch to his voice gave away his excitement.

"Well, Russ, we just followed your directions, that's all."

"Yes, but which way did you go?"

"Right up the trail like you said."

Our voices elevated a bit.

"What was it like?"

"It was just like you said, except you guys left some artifacts there, didn't you?"

We got a bit louder! Russell did some huffing and puffing but he would not admit that Ben was the one that actually found the camp, and I did not mention the mine.

Anyway, we were both upset. He finally went out and slammed the makeshift screen door as if he were going home. He came right back in when he remembered he *was* home.

Of course that wasn't the end of our adventures with Panamint Russell.

LOST GOLD, SIX SPRINGS

Once when Benny Williams and I were at Russell's camp, and no one was around to interrupt us, we sat at the little round kitchen table in the cook shack, and he told me about a young man who had come into camp one day and asked him to help him.

Now, as I have said before, Benny was just the opposite of Russell. Benny wasn't a blowhard and he was very truthful. When he was telling me this story I could see he was still very emotional about it.

Benny said, "Not too long ago a young man, George Jensen, drove into camp while I was here alone and he had quite a tale. He told me that before WWII, when he was a teenager that he had been with his father and some other members of his family when they had gone on a prospecting trip up into these Panamint Mountains. He said that they had gone into Six Springs Canyon."

"Now that big canyon is steep and rugged and it drains to the east down into the floor of Death Valley. Do you know where it is?" he asked me. At that time I only had a vague idea that it was not many miles to the north from where we were. Benny continued, "If you drive as far north here in Butte Valley as you can you will end up near Arrastre Spring, an old Indian hangout. Then if you climb up over the ridge that closes off the north end of the valley you will be able to get into the upper part of Six Springs Canyon. You can, of course, go down into the floor of Death Valley and come up from the lower end of the canyon, too, but it's a long way to get to the springs that way.

"Anyway, this young man, George, he tells me that on their trip the people he was with treated him like so much dirt. Like a servant. They didn't want him with them, and they left him and took off from camp, leaving him behind with orders for him to clean out a nearby spring."

He said he worked hard digging and cleaning out brush, then in the afternoon he found some pieces of raw gold, little nuggets, scattered around not far from the spring he had been working on.

View shows Striped Butte in the foreground and the north end of the valley in the background to the right of the butte where Arrastré Springs is located. Photo by author.

Well, George must have felt very bad about the way he was being treated by his dad and his friends, because he told me that he kept his discovery secret.

"George told me that he had left home and joined the army and had gone away for a long time and now he had come back to go back to that spring and find more gold. He felt sure that he could find the same place again. He said that the glow of that hidden treasure had spurred him on several times when he had been in a tight spot.

He showed me a piece of gold he said he had found at the spring those many years before. And he asked me to go with him and help him. At the time I wasn't well. I wanted to go with him but I really felt bad and I asked him if he could wait a day or two until I was feeling better.

No, he was too excited and he couldn't wait. He drove off alone and I watched his sedan disappear as a column of dust trailed behind it on the road up the valley."

"I was anxious to see how he made out and I was still waiting to hear from him a few days later. I was a lot better then, and I was just getting ready to go see if I could find out what happened to George when a Ranger drove up. He asked me if I knew anything about the car that someone had found abandoned up near Arrastre Springs.

I told him everything that I could. A search party climbed over into the canyon where he was supposed to have gone, but they found no trace of him. They searched up from the floor of the valley too. I have never heard of anyone finding anything yet. I sure wish I had been able to go with him or that he would have waited a day or so."

I believe Benny died in the early 1960s without learning about the fate of George.

My two sons and I, as well, tried to find some trace of George and his gold but we didn't have any luck either.

Arrastré Springs, location of a Spanish style gold mill. Photo by author.

BENNY WILLIAMS' UNTIMELY DEATH

In the early 1960s Panamint Russell and Clinton Anderson teamed up. Now I was not really involved with either of them at the time as I was busy in and out doing my prospecting and so the story of what happened came to me in bits and pieces. Carl Ruona was a little closer with what was going on around Russell's camp then. However, what happened affected me deeply because I did like Benny and I had talked with him more than any of the rest of them. So here's what I remember:

Russell, God bless him, was of course, among his other talents, a first-class con man. And most of us know that con men are, by nature, easily taken in by other con men. And so the more I learned about Clinton's and Russell's alliance, I was convinced it was a perfect example of this phenomenon.

Clinton, as I recall, was an engineer of some sort, who had worked at the Jet Propulsion Laboratory in Pasadena, California. I remember his wife Stella once told me that Clinton's name was on some piece of hardware that had been landed on the moon. He had hi-tech skills that Russell did not understand. However Russell did believe that Clinton could build them a device that could detect bodies of rich underground mineral deposits, using radar (today this can be done to some degree, maybe Clinton was just way ahead of his time).

Some speculated that there might have been some misappropriations of J.P.L equipment. At least Clinton was no longer working at the laboratory when he and Russell began to put together their Radar Machine. I was told that Russell had rented a garage to store the surplus Army radar trailer that they had acquired. And Clinton was busy redesigning the device in order to make it into something that would allow them to pinpoint all of the rich veins of gold and silver that Russell had told Clinton about. These were plentiful within a mile or two of his camp. Russell had even shown him places that his psychic friends had pointed out.

When I first saw Clinton and Stella Anderson, I was given
to believe that they were to be held in great esteem. I think Russell
thought that Clinton might be compared to the famous White
Sands, New Mexico, developer Dr. Robert Oppenheimer. Clinton
sort of dressed the part anyway. There was certainly quite a bit of
mutual respect between the two men.

That is where the trouble started, not enough respect to go
around.

Although Benny Williams would not lock the place up like
Russell wanted and he left a log book on the table for visitors, he
had, for many years, taken care of the camp when Russell wasn't
there. It was because of Benny's support that Russell had been
able to maintain his latter-day "Death Valley Scotty" image, while
he was working as a guard for the Power and Light Company in
Los Angeles. This project was going to allow Russell to be able
to retire to his mine camp in his old age.

Benny was older and had some health problems, and even
though he had a place to stay near Trona, he loved the desert and
the peacefulness of the camp high in the Panamints. When I first
met Benny I was told that he and Russell had been partners for
many years.

But things changed when Clinton showed up. Then Benny
was expected not only to take a back seat; he was also called
upon to be Clinton's "Man Friday."

For years Russell had brought to camp anything he could
get away with from the Power and Light Company. He had col-
lected many miles of copper wire. Hundreds of rolls. His dream
was to string a phone wire seven miles over the mountain ridges
between his camp and Myers camp in upper Goler Wash.

Clinton decided that he would start out their bonanza project.
Benny already had a phone line but it was only a few hundred
feet long. It went between Russell's camp and the Greater View
Springs camp. This deluxe service had an old-style crank phone
at either end, but now Clinton was there and they were going to
put in the new modern service.

In order to reach the ridgeline where the wire was to be

strung, it required a very steep, several-hundred-feet climb up from camp.

On a warm day, and without making a trail, Clinton had the old man start hauling rolls of wire up to the ridge while he started stringing wire from boulder to boulder. By the end of the day Benny was exhausted and ill.

I happened by the next day. Clinton was gone, but Benny told me what they had been doing.

He said that he felt awful. It looked to me like he had a heart attack. I wanted to take him down to the little chemical-plant hospital in Trona but he said he felt too bad to make the trip. So I stayed there with him for a couple of days. By then though he said that he felt much better and he didn't want to go to town.

The next time I was around, Carl told me that Benny had ended up in the hospital anyway and that, yes, it had been a heart attack he was suffering from.

When Benny was released from the hospital, he was told to stay out of the mountains. However it wasn't too long before he was back up in Striped Butte Valley at Russell's camp. By then it was fall and it was getting very cold at that high elevation at night. One evening, the Andersons rolled into camp and they needed Benny's room to stay in.

Benny slept out in the cold in front of the cabin on an old canvas army cot. In the morning, just when the first light began to bring out the many brilliant colors of the Black and the Funeral ranges to the east, Benny slowly rose from his cot. There were frosty patches, here and there, like fragile doilies. He opened the door to the cook shack, walked in and fell dead on the round table, the round table that had been pivotal to many of our camp meetings and stories—the same table where Benny kept his logbook.

This created a dilemma for a while, that is until they were able to get Benny set up in the front seat of the Anderson car and take him down to the paved road in the floor of Death Valley where the coroner could pick him up.

The Andersons had a place to stay from then on. They eventually bought the Greater View camp next door from Sid Waley and became permanent residents for many years. Stella even stayed on for years after Clinton died in a Veterans Hospital in Long Beach, California. As I understand it, he died as the result of a strange camp accident.

Both Stella and Clinton were not the kind of people that you would expect to find living in such remote country. They were afraid of things that go bump in the night. They always kept a guard dog tied to the bed at night and they would not go out in the dark for any reason. And strange as it seems, that is what killed Clinton. You see, Stella told me he got an infection from cutting himself while urinating into a rusty tin can.

Anyway, Russell, after Benny died, always had someone to baby-sit his camp whenever he was gone. Stella would come over from next door. She never left any doors unlocked!

Russell still had something to gripe about though; it seemed that she tried to eat him out of house and home anytime she stayed there. "By God, Emmett, she had to have the best of everything too, fresh meat, no pork and beans for her, no sir."

I was unforgiving about Benny's death. It was many years before I would have anything to do with the Anderson's, but as the years passed, I finally decided that I was now being the jerk. Clinton and Stella had become fixtures in Butte Valley. No, the radar machine never quite got perfected and their circumstances seemed to be slim at best. By then people had started to try to look after them a bit.

Campers would stop by on the way out and leave off any extra food that they had left, or sometimes other camp supplies. At last, I decided to go by their place on my way out. No one had been around for a while so I stopped to ask Stella what she would like from town. "I really love okra," she said. On my next trip in I proudly brought a dozen cans of okra for her. She said, "Oh, no, Emmett, I only eat *fresh* okra!"

Those cans sat on the shelf at my camp for a long time. I kept hoping someone would steal them and someone did, finally.

THE VACATION

I would leave my half-ton 1950 GMC van (nicknamed the Green Machine) at the ghost town of Ballarat. This spot in the lonely desert, the archeological ruins of an old western mining town, had melted adobe walls on either side of the once righteous main street. There were a few buildings still standing, one or two still had a roof and could be used for shelter. There was a new (less that ten years old) building at the end of the main street. It had been built by a developer that had dreamt of starting a desert trailer park. The park had not happened and the Jones family had conned the owner into letting them live (squat) there.

Paul Jones was a special character. In the desert, as you know, it's normal to meet a variety of characters, but Paul was head and shoulders beyond the average. He and his wife, Lilian, with their two small children, Paul Jr. and Little Lilian, were operating a kitchen and store there. It was an oasis for the explorers and prospectors that ventured off the paved highway and made their way across the dry lake that bordered the old mining town on the west. There was a smooth, elevated dirt road that bisected the lakebed in a straight line.

This family led by Paul, with his enterprising ways, survived quite well there. They not only provided services at the store building, but they were always ready to assist anyone that they could, to overcome any difficulties that they might get into in that remote desert area. And of course, as good Samaritans, they would ordinarily collect, one way or another, a monetary reward for their kindness.

Paul and Lillian are gone now and in telling this story I have taken the liberty of changing the names so as not to embarrass the survivors, including myself. So I will use the term so often used now and say this story is based on what really happened.

Ballarat, a place where you leave the modern world behind, where you step off into the mysteries of Death Valley, is the last outpost, the last touch with civilization, until you cross the Panamint Mountains and get to the floor of Death Valley. Over a hundred miles away, barren land, rocky, gorgeous fragile desert flora and fauna, majestic colors, a land saturated by the aura of the old west.

When I would head for the mine that way, instead of coming in from the east side of Death Valley, I was in the habit of leaving my Green Machine there at the ghost town. I had a WWII surplus four-wheel drive Dodge Army truck, unlicensed; that I left there, paying Paul a small fee or sometimes I would bring him a load of old mounted tires from my brother's wrecking yard. He did quite well in the tire business. The combination of city folk and rock strewn desert roads provided Paul marvelous opportunities to be a hero to many travelers in Panamint Valley.

The Vacation Story started one cool winter morning many years ago when I pulled into Ballarat, on my way to the mine; it was early Friday morning.

"Hi Emmett, going up to Butte Valley?"

"Yes Paul, I'm in a hurry, I've got some things to do up there and then I have to get right back down town by Monday. How's Lilian and the kids?"

"Well," And as he hesitated, he looked wistfully at the back of my panel truck. The cool winter breeze came across the stark lakebed like random spirits gliding through the interruptions that had once been a booming mining town in the not too distant past. The spirits formed small whirlwinds that danced about us as we stood there between the van and the Dodge mine truck. The quiet and the chill were the perfect setting for what was about to take place.

Paul looked down, and in a voice that was unmistakably the voice of a poor man, down on his luck and up against a hard place, he said:

"Well, Emmett, it is sure getting cold here now. The kids are complaining. We're almost out of firewood and that big old propane tank, well—it's too big. I don't have anything running that I can haul it in. If I could get it into Trona I could get it filled and the kids would be sure grateful, you know! Flu-season is coming on, you know?"

When I did not answer right away, Paul went on,

"It's only 25 miles, in and back. I would not be gone long. Can you help us out?"

Well what could I say, all I could do was pray he could make it into town and back without running over someone or wrecking my work truck. After all it was the time of year to be grateful and Christian. And the children were cold.

"Sure Paul, that big tank will fit in there, be sure and tie it down good though—and hook the back doors somehow, you won't be able to close them all the way."

"I might be down any time," I said, so as to inspire him to be prudent about his trip to town.

I had misgivings; I had this visceral feeling—yes, paranoia is a constant companion for those who travel alone in the desert, but I was a rational person.

Anyway, as I drove the mine truck south out of the ghost town, in the rearview mirror, wind devils swirled around the store building and around my "Green Machine." That truck and I had been through many adventures together. It had been a friend indeed. Many a cold rainy night, or scorching summer day, like a desert space ship it had brought me back from the moon. "Oh well the truck would be all right, letting Paul use it was a Christian gesture," I was talking to myself again.

The town disappeared, hidden by the bold rocky point of the mountains that protrudes out into the lakebed south of the metropolis. I soon let go of my trepidation, and it was replaced with the proper warm spot in my chest—it was after all, the Yuletide.

It was Sunday morning when I got back. It was still cold and dusty in Ballarat. I felt good; I had climbed to the Mormon mine and brought back a heavy pack of rich specimen ore.

Wind devils, yes, but no smoke from the store building. And where in hell was my van?

The Jones children were huddled inside the store building, the propane tank was still empty. "Where's your mom and dad?"

Cheerily Tammy answered, "Emmett, they went on vacation!"

"What! They went on vacation?"

My voice became very subdued, a monotone, quite.

"Where did they go?"

"Oh, I think they went to Reno, Nevada," the little girl smiled brightly again; mature beyond her years, she was happy for mom and dad. Tom added, "Yeah, I think that's where they said they were going."

"When will they be back?"

Little Lilian, still smiling, "I don't know, they didn't say."

I stood under the store porch roof, looking at the bleak dried mud flat. It shimmered even in the cool winter air. It was a long two miles across the lake now; I would have to leave the mine truck here; I could not leave it out by the paved road. As the old prospector Harry Briggs would say, "It would be Shank's mare from here—walking." I was "afoot" now like so many of the old timers that used to come and go when Ballarat was in its heyday.

Because it was winter there were no visitors in Ballarat all day. I spent the day working on the mine truck doing "catch up maintenance." When the shadows started to blend and dusk descended I wondered where I would camp, it looked like I would spend a cold night on the hard bed of the truck; the wind was picking up. And just then another pickup came rattling down out of the mountains into town.

That was the first time I met George Goodwin, a single-burro (or at least a single pickup) prospector like myself. I had heard of him before and George was working a small mine up a canyon not far from Ballarat. Lucky for me George also was the proud owner of one of the livable shacks in Ballarat. He invited me to spend the night on a cot in his place. We settled in and enjoyed his glowing little makeshift stove—a steel barrel turned sideways with sturdy stove pipe fastened to it.

After I got over squawking, like the proverbial mashed cat, about what had happened to my van and we had discussed the fact that I could not file a stolen vehicle report (after all Paul had my permission to use the van), George and I talked far into the night on more pleasant topics; we had a lot in common and shared some of our personal mining stories.

In the morning George offered to take me to the highway but I was caught up in the nostalgia of the old west, and I guess I was wallowing a little in the role of a masochist.

I said, "Thanks, George, for your hospitality, I've enjoyed meeting you, but I know that you just came down to get your mail that Paul was supposed to bring back from town. No, I'll wait till later, and then I'll walk out to the pavement. By then I think there will be some cars going into Trona, maybe I'll catch a ride."

In the store the Jones kids had coffee going. After breakfast, as we were making small talk, the boy said, "I think someone is coming, see the dust on the lake road." There was a large pair of field glasses on the windowsill. With the image in focus—low and behold, there was my Green Machine. There was a large house trailer following close behind.

My emotions were mixed; I was thrilled, all my visions of many vehicular calamities vaporized, but on the other hand, I was stunned that they had the nerve to pull this stunt. And now there was my precious truck pulling a load three times too big for it.

"There goes the clutch." Talking to myself again. What about the new Ford 3/4-ton truck following in the dust cloud billowing about the Green Machine and the house trailer?"

"Emmett, It's good to see you!"

Paul slapped me on the back. I was sitting on the counter stool seething; I held my tongue and controlled my desire to punch him in the face. I guess I was overpowered—amazed, by the colossal nerve being exhibited. This was Paul Jones, practicing his special skill, a sort of dark magic I suppose.

"Let me introduce you to John Blakesfield." My reply was restrained, "Hello, John."

"Glad to meet you Emmett. Boy! We were real lucky, my wife and I—she's in the trailer right now. Yes we were pulling our new trailer over Walker Pass and it was too much for the Ford and then here comes Paul Jones and his wonderful old truck and saves the day! The Ford, the transmission is going out, think it might make it to town without the trailer. Paul has volunteered to look after the trailer till we can get back."

John and Paul went on to congratulate each other on their

adventure. John Blakesfield, of course, forced a wad of money into Paul's hand. Paul turned to me, his ruddy Irish complexion aglow, and peeled off fifteen dollars for me, being very obvious in his generous act.

"Thanks a lot, Emmett—you may need some gas." Still smiling, he tucked my reward into my shirt pocket.

WILL ROPER

The Striped Butte was a beautiful multicolored backdrop when Will and his buddy pulled off the dusty trail into a natural clearing. Around the open space there were several pale green, pungent, creosote bushes. They were there to prospect and look for a gold mine. They unloaded the Ford truck and set up camp quickly. Will told me that they had seen no signs of anyone anywhere in the valley when they got there. This was way back, he never told me exactly when it was; however, I would guess from other things he said it must have been in the late 20s or early 30s.

The coffee was done and they were about to start cooking their meal when a big guy came into their camp and poured himself a cup of coffee. If Will told me where this guy came from I don't remember. If he had a car Will didn't say. Anyway, this big tough-looking hombre looked everything over carefully as he stood there drinking their brew. Then he said, "Well, boys, I am going to take all your gear." Will said, "He was just sort of matter-of-fact about it, quite sure of himself."

Will was sitting on a campstool, as was his buddy and they looked at each other stunned. Mister Big was quite serious and he kicked over the fire, picked up a burlap bag and started gathering up their grub and things. As he worked he would glance in their direction now and then. "This was no joke, if looks would kill he would have done us both in right there," Will told me.

He said that his knapsack was right beside the stool he was sitting on, and he had a chrome-plated revolver in it. He said he swallowed hard, held his breath, and reached for the gun. His hand was shaking and the hammer on the gun made a loud click as he pulled it back—he didn't think he could miss; it was point blank. Mister Big only started to turn when the loud report rippled across Striped Butte Valley.

Will told me that he and his friend dug the grave and buried the intruder right there not far from the road near the middle of the butte.

He said, "That was a long time ago and we were so scared

that I buried that chrome-plated pistol in the yard at the Greater View camp south of the butte. I suppose it is still there."

Years after Will Roper died in Goler Wash of a heart attack I told his story to a young man who was living in the stone (1860) house at Greater View. He prowled around digging here and there and he came up with an old chrome pistol. So I gave Will's story a little more credence after that.

I first met Mr. Roper in Striped Butte Valley while Carl and I were working there. Will had been in and around the area for a good number of years. This time he was there because he had made a deal to live at the Myers well-stocked and well-maintained camp in Goler Wash, upstream from the little shack the

On the other side of the butte near the road is where Will Roper said he buried the body. Photo by Ron McKinley.

Manson Family would make famous years later. Will was staying in a small one-room cabin to the rear of the main house at the camp.

He was a decent, interesting person, and even though his

serious heart problem disabled him quite a bit he still could get around fairly well. Will was not small, he looked strong, his hair was gray and he wore glasses that made him look distinguished.

One of the reasons he had made the deal with the Myers family to stay at the camp as their caretaker was that he knew of a secret gold mine on Manly Peak nearby. Now his heart prevented him from climbing that 7,000-foot mountain; however, he still wanted to be near the action. He and Carl got to be good friends for quite a while and they told me about the rich gold mine he was looking for.

Will Roper had first learned about the mine when he lived in Las Vegas, Nevada many years before. While there he became good friends with a fellow who was quite a gambler and he always had a good deal of money. This friend finally confided in Will that his secret was that every couple of months he would go into the mountains at the south end of Death Valley and bring back some rich gold ore, almost pure gold. He said, "I can go up there and get what I need in one day. I go up to the mine, it's on the south end of Manly Peak, and come right back down with enough to last me for months."

Before Will could learn exactly where this mine was, in Las Vegas one dark night in a back alley, someone robbed and murdered his buddy. Even though that had been many years ago, Will still was sure his friend was telling him the truth and that rich vein of gold was there and the ghost of the gambler was pulling him toward it.

Will and Carl spent some time stomping around that end of the mountain, but I don't think they found much. It was during that time that Carl got us in trouble with the Department of Interior when he used a small bulldozer he had bought and brought up there to fix up a small stretch of one of the old prospector roads, but that's another story.

While Will was staying at the Myers', the Keystone mine was operating in Goler Wash, down canyon from him a few miles. They were mining gold.

It was during this time when Will got this idea to fix up his old Jeep. He was going to modify it and put a regular automobile body on it. I thought it was a crazy idea but with some help from the boys at the mine he came out with a respectable machine.

He enjoyed his Jeep "Deluxe" for several weeks before calamity struck.

Will told me, "One evening I was going to run to town and the Jeep wouldn't start so I tried to get it going by rolling it down the wash in front of the camp.

The bottom of the wash there is loose sand and not much of a grade. I kept struggling to get it rolling and then I would jump in, but each time it didn't turn over enough to start. When I got clear down by Sourdough Spring my heart gave out and I collapsed. I took my pills but I could hardly move, little by little I crawled back up the wash. It took me the rest of the night to drag myself up to my cabin. I got the door open, crawled next to the stove, reached up and turned all four burners on. When the shack warmed up enough, I was able to get into the big overstuffed chair. I was so weak I couldn't even light a cigarette. It was evening the next day before I could get up."

This is the cabin Will Roper lived in at the Meyers Camp. Photo by Ron McKinley.

When he told me his story it had been three weeks back that this had happened and he looked great. He had been busy, driving back and forth between his camp and the widow Stella Anderson's camp at Greater View Springs. It had become Will's lot to see that she was all right. This was before a ten-year-old boy, Bobbie, was dropped off at her camp. Then as I saw it, Bobbie became her slave.

Meantime down at the Keystone Mine the miners had expected Will to come by the mine Wednesday on his way to town, but he didn't show up. Thursday they went up to check on him. All four burners of his stove were still on when they found him in the big chair. This time he didn't live to tell any more stories. I guess he and the Gambler are still guarding that high-grade mine on the south end of Manly Peak.

It was Saturday, Stella's birthday, when Will made his last trip to town to bring her supplies. She bragged to me that she had fixed Will his last supper. Me, I wondered what she fed him and I declined her next dinner invitation.

MR. BRIGGS

During my Death Valley days I came to know one of the last old-timers quite well. He became my mentor, and he had a great deal of influence on my adventures in the badlands. It is with a great deal of respect that I introduce "Mr. Briggs" in this chapter.

※

On the way to our *"diggins"* if we came in from the west side of Death Valley, we would travel on the old road that runs north and south in Panamint Valley. It skirts the edge of the ancient dry lakebed. It was once a stagecoach route to connect with other gold mining towns. The ghost town of Ballarat, laid out in 1897, is situated along that road. It is nestled into the alluvium of the Panamints at the effluence of Pleasant Canyon. The site that would become Ballarat was probably sighted from points in the Panamints as early as 1849 by the Mormon Jayhawker (Manley-Bennett-Arcane) party when they broke out of Death Valley. It would not become the town site of Ballarat until 1897 as a result of much mining activity in the area starting in the 1870s.

Ballarat was almost passed up in favor of Post Office Springs just a mile or so away but the marshy ground around the spring was thought not to be suitable for a "main street". Ballarat came into being when it was decided to move the two saloons and grocery from the Ratcliff Mine in Pleasant Canyon to the flats below, where a town would have room to grow.

William Caruthers in his book, *Loafing Along Death Valley Trails,* gives this account of the naming: "When the citizens met to choose a name, George Riggins, a young Australian, suggested the new town be given a name identified with gold the world over. Ballarat in his native country met the requirement and its name was adopted."

A1901 cloudburst nearly destroyed all the buildings and then competing gold boomtowns drew away a lot of the population. Even so Ballarat has stayed with us. For almost 25 years it was a typical western mining town. There were stages, freight wagons and all varieties of buggies, mules, horses and so forth, traveling to and from this bustling metropolis. The town and some of the mines in the area lasted long enough to see automobiles take over. And as happened in so many towns that came with the glitter of gold the dream faded slowly. Oh, there were short periods when new prospects would shine, however the world kind of turned its back on Ballarat. The Radcliff, O. B. Joyful, the Anthony and the Cooper mines had produced over a million in gold and then they all finally shut down. Eventually the two-story hotel in Ballarat, and most everything else except Boot Hill disappeared.

In the late 1950s when we were going in or out from our base camp in Butte Valley, we would sometimes go through Ballarat. At that time there was one modern building left amongst the melting adobe walls of this now forgotten boomtown. This newer building had been built by Mr. Cummings who bought the whole ghost town a few years before we started going that way.

He had hoped to make Ballarat rise from its ashes, so to speak. He had wanted to develop it as a modern trailer park. Finances and a variety of other circumstances prevented the fulfillment of his dream. He has relatives buried in the cemetery on the edge of town. I guess the graves there and the grave of the famous prospector, "Seldom Seen Slim", helps to verify that this place is a "By God Ghost Town." Before Cummings came, for years, "Seldom Seen Slim" (Charles Ferge) had been the sole inhabitant of this waning town.

Cumming's building, the start of his trailer park, is like an apparition amongst the forlorn remnants along the main street. It has bathrooms and a shower, and sometimes electricity. Almost always there is someone there. The building today is a store, and Louie (The Mayor) runs it. Cliff

"Seldom Seen Slim",
Charles Ferge, about 1967.
Photo by author.

Walker (Western Historian and denizen of the desert), last year, after he came back from visiting Australia, presented Louie with a letter from the mayor of the "Aussie" town of Ballarat. They are sister cities only in name. Ballarat, Australia is now a large bustling town, while the ghost town here sometimes sports a population of two or three; but Louie has this "sister city" letter prominently displayed on the wall in the store.

Typical of many of the old west ghost towns, there is still a small society of special people that gravitate to less complicated lifestyles. At times they can be found hovering around in the dust of this town of a thousand bygone hurrahs. When Slim died in 1968 a national television crew came to town for his funeral and there was a big turn out.

When we would stop by Ballarat, we would hear some locals telling stories, or making comments, about Harry Briggs.

Through the course of this eavesdropping we learned that Mr. Briggs was a very independent fellow and that he had a camp in the Panamint foothills, south, halfway between Ballarat and

Headstone of "Seldom Seen Slim" Charles Ferge in Ballarat's boot hill cemetery. His epitaph reads: "Me lonely? Hell no! I'm half coyote and half burro." Photo by Ron McKinley.

the Goler Wash turn-off. And even though Harry had been mining in Panamint Valley longer than any other living soul, he did not hang out with the "Who hit John? (bad whiskey)" crowd that sometimes gathered at Ballarat. They really didn't know much about him even though Slim had a cabin down there and would sometimes prospect the hills above Briggs' camp (more about the Ballarat boys and girls later).

Harry's camp, some distance on down the valley, was a little way off to the east of the road, situated right at the mouth of Redlands Canyon. There had been a mill site located there in 1894, when some of the early prospectors in these desolate mountains needed to process gold ore from a nearby claim. Old mining records verified this. In fact, Redlands Canyon had become noteworthy even earlier than that. This narrow, picturesque canyon had been the escape route for some of the hapless members of the lost 1849 pioneer wagon train. These struggling survivors were responsible for Death Valley ending up with such a foreboding name.

We would pass the dirt road that turned off to Harry's place each time we used the Panamint Valley road. The trace of this driveway made its way around the larger boulders and through gullies, climbing up the alluvium, ending at the old mill site. As we would go by, I'd wonder about this mystery man, what kind of a desert denizen was he? His driveway was over a quarter of a mile long. Far off at the end, right up against the base of the mountains, you could see a small bunch of trees. Of course, that rare spot of green stood out boldly in this drab, brown, bleak, countryside.

Asa Russell and others, in Butte Valley, higher in the range near our camp, knew little about Harry or his doings. Panamint Russell knew everything there was to know about everything, but when I pressed him or his friends for details about Harry they'd clam up, they didn't have an inside track on him and his Southern Homestead mine.

As it turned out, Harry's camp had a small following of its own. But most of his friends were more into mining than they were into swapping stories about bygone times.

I was intrigued. The vague stories I had heard about Harry said he was quite ornery and very self-reliant. Now, as I saw myself as a modern-day "Lost Dutchman," I was prone to keep a low profile, not wanting anyone to know too much about my travels or activities since it was safer that way: I saw Mr. Briggs as a kindred soul.

Also, I had come to understand that it was possible to put some of the local folklore together, from different camps, and with a little research of the old mining records I could walk historical paths that others might not see. I might even find more hidden treasures. The more I thought about it the more important it became for me to know Mr. Briggs.

By airline miles, his camp, on lower slopes of the Panamint, was close to Russell's Camp and even closer to my Aluminum Cabin. But actually there was a lot of mountain in between and the difference in elevation was dramatic. By road it was well over an hour and a half between my camp and Harry's. A road looping around the southern end of the range and then back up though the spine on the west side of Death Valley was some of the most difficult you ever wanted to travel.

One sunny day on my way out, I was coming down Goler Wash alone in my "Green Machine." It was a 1950 GMC ½-ton van. I had bought this van from my brother's wrecking yard and it had a few dings and scratches and I was not worried about compromising its beauty in this rough and tumble country. The road was bad as usual. It had been a slow trip, because I would stop here and there to work on the road, like we all did in those days. I was headed to Ballarat. It was about noontime when I got out in the valley to where you could see the Briggs Camp. As the van, with its steady beat, skirted the dry lakebed I was prompted by some visceral notion to turn toward his place.

Halfway up, there was a rusty iron gate, a long pipe framework that blocked the road completely. There were piles of large rocks and gullies on either side, no chance to drive around it. After getting out to look over this obstacle, I could see that on up at the camp there were at least three smaller buildings and a larger one in among the salt cedar trees, forming sort of a compound. It was still a ways to the camp but it looked like someone might be there. Through trees in front of the larger building, I thought I could see a pickup truck.

The gate had an open lock hanging from a chain (I was to learn that the key for the lock was always stuck under a rock at the pivot end of the gate). I swung the pipe uphill and fastened it out of the way, drove through and then got out and closed it behind me. I drove past the pale green International four-wheel drive pickup and parked at the north end of the main building in the shade of the trees. Mr. Briggs walked up as I climbed out of the van. In my hand I had a paper sack with a few boiled eggs and some crackers and an orange. My lunch.

When I introduced myself, he said, "I've heard about you, Emmett. I'm glad to meet you."

"I have a sack of victuals, how about some lunch," I said.

"Thanks, I've already et. How about I get us some libation, O.K.?" He went to a Servel (It ran on bottled gas) refrigerator in the shade under the lean-to porch roof beside us. He came back with two bottles.

He was an old man in his late 70s, but lithe and trim. His hair was thin and though you could tell he was no stranger to the sun his complexion was fair. He was wearing a blue denim shirt and khaki pants.

"Here, have some vitamin pee," he said as he handed me a bottle of beer.

I was sitting on the running board of my van peeling an egg and Harry drug up a salvaged, old pre-WWII, metal lawn chair. As we talked it was obvious that even though there was a wide spread in our ages we had a lot in common. Harry loved this country and he loved prospecting. This was one of my luckiest days. This meeting was the start of a great friendship. I had struck gold again.

Harry and I ended up working together on several projects. I had the opportunity to spend many nights at one or another of his camps (he had two more mill sites higher up in the mountains). I still miss those nights, sitting in a well-weathered clapboard mine shack, hearing the whistle of the Coleman lantern announcing its glow and listening to Harry talking. Within the circle of limited light it was as if we were lost in sort of a time warp. We talked and talked. I was fortunate; I appreciated these

Harry Briggs on left with the author taken about 1967. Photo by Ruth Harder.

windows into the past. I made a tape recording of several of our talks (when listening to any of these tapes you can tell if my wife was present, Harry's vocabulary improved if she was there. He was always a gentleman whenever there were any ladies within earshot).

He, like many older people I have talked to or read about, could remember remarkable details, even from his earliest childhood. He could still remember a youthful, dreadful episode. I can still hear him laughing as he shared his story with me.

"I remember I was too young to go to school, by God, and I know that livin' up there in Kansas—Barnard, Kansas, my dad was down there on Salt Creek and I know I went to school with my oldest brother and sister. I was too young to go to school so I must have been about four but I went along with them. I went to

Picture of "high-graders" cleanup crew at the Banti Mine, Harry Briggs with Ruth Harder. Photo by the author.

the outhouse and I had bad luck, I mussed myself all up. I wouldn't go back into the schoolhouse, but I started walking home. And I walked for a long ways, and there a woman come along in the buggy, and she said, 'Little boy, do you want a ride.' I said 'No thanks lady, I'd just as soon walk.' Now I walked on home and I wasn't smellin' very good and I was settin' on the porch and this woman had come up to visit my mother. And this lady come out of the house and I was just settin' down off the porch, ya know, 'Why' she says, 'that's the little boy I wanted to give a ride! Who's little boy is that?' And mama says, 'Why that's my little boy!' I remember that just as plain as today."

Another story about his youth he shared one night in camp. I can still hear his voice,

"I remember my grandfather lived up in Beloit, Kansas, a big guy, been a Captain in the 32nd Indiana Calvary, Civil War. We went a fishin', Salt Creek half mile from the house. There's this great big warty toad, ya know ya seen them? He said 'Pick it up an' bring it along'. I was kind of hesitant; I said I'd get warts on me. 'Naw that's all bunk, that won't get no warts on ya.' I brought the toad along and he just hooked the hook through his back and set a pole there in the crick. The crick was runnin' high and we went down the next mornin' and we had a channel catfish that was close to three foot long. The damndest fish I ever saw!"

As a young man Harry started out farming, like his dad and his brothers. They rented land and put in crops each season. The family worked together and they paid each other wages for the work they put in on their separate farms. Then one year there wasn't enough rain, that, with an early hot spell, the wheat was so poor that after he settled up and paid everyone he didn't have enough left to seed back. He decided to head out west on his own.

 He staked out a piece of land and worked hard to clear it. Some of the sagebrush was taller than a man, with stalks as big as a small tree. He was inspired by the fact that his dad promised him that if he got himself set up he would furnish him with his own herd of cattle. But by the time he came home to get the cattle he found out his dad had died and the family farm had been split up.

For a while he made his way as a cowboy. He spent months with a partner off in the hills rounding up wild cattle for a big outfit. I remember him saying, "Them westerns they make now are all bunk, when we'd come in off the range, we didn't race to the bar, we'd go right to the grocery store ta get ourselves a can of peaches, that's what we were a craving."

Then he got bit by the bug—he went to work in one of the big gold mines, as a mucker making big money, three dollars a day. After a while he moved up to being a driller.

When WWI came along he joined the army and ended up in

England as an airplane mechanic.

After he got home from the war the big oil rush started in the Midwest. The Oklahoma Crude black gold rush. Harry was in on the ground floor. During this bonanza he ended up as CEO of an oil company. It was rough and tumble wild times then. Harry was right there in the middle of it driving a Stutz Bearcat sports car. He was caught up in a whirlwind of money, working day and night.

Then Katy lowered the boom. Mrs. Briggs, the demure and crippled little girl he had married during leaner years, according to Harry, was working nights too, while he was away. Their divorce could not have hit the courts in a worse time. When the National Banks went berserk, and the 1930s depression swept the land, all of Harry's assets were tied up. He lost everything. He wasn't even able to pay his family (his brother and sister worked for him in his oil field) the wages he owed them.

Harry Briggs was almost eighty years old when I first met him. He had a small income from social security but always supplemented that. He was a doer all of his life. After he had come west his gold fever took a good hold on him.

Harry did tell me an amusing story about the time, a year or so after he first came west. He had run out of luck and money and decided to quit mining and prospecting. He drove away from the mine camp in the Panamint Mountains in his old Model T Ford (a far cry from the Stutz Bearcat he had in the oil fields) and headed for Los Angeles.

He didn't get far, only to the Slate Range pass on the far side of Panamint Valley, where an old dirt road made by Chinese labor crossed over.

"Right there the old Model T truck blew a tire, cur-bam, plop, and I was out of spares. There was some moonlight but I decided to wait for daylight to look for an old discarded piece of tire that I could make a boot out of to fix the flat. Well, while I was sitting there bein' glum I see this car come out from Trona way, but it stopped at the little dry lake at the bottom of the pass. There was light enough to see what that couple was doin'.

They was gone in the mornin' and I walked down the road

to the lakebed and I not only found a old tire, but there was a big fat shiny wallet layin' in the dust where that car had been. Well, Emmett, there I had a new grubstake and I been here ever since."

There was another time, way back when Harry Porter and Harry Briggs got into it at this same pass. Mr. Porter was the luckiest prospector in the whole area. He found himself a gold mine way up on what is now called Porter Peak. His small mine would produce quartz that was half gold. And even though he had a new car, he loved his burros. One day he came into Ballarat leading one of his animals and Harry Porter had a pack on his back and the burro didn't, when someone asked him why, he said, "My burro doesn't feel good."

Anyway at the pass, Harry Briggs who was still relatively a young man, a red-headed young man with a temper, crossed trails with Harry Porter. Now Mr. Porter, who was much older, had a pretty good temper of his own and he had heard that Harry Briggs had one of his missing burros and had been using it at his mine. They got into it then and there. They were both wearing six-guns and they both slapped leather as they say. If their companions had not grabbed the guns someone would have been shot. Harry Briggs told me, "Some of his burros had come into my camp one snowy night and I just hadn't got around to sending them home yet, that's all."

Harry and I got to be good friends and he became my mentor and a father figure. My wife and Harry got on well; he was quite gallant when the three of us would go out to dinner.

Even though Russell's and Briggs' camps were only a few airline miles from each other, they lived on different sides of the mountain, conceptually as well as physically. They never liked each other. Briggs thought Russell was an old blow-hard. Briggs being a successful miner was enough for Russell to dislike him. When I would compare or combine their different stories about the area it was like magic, I could hear a faint voice whispering, "Now, Emmett, take a new look at some of those old trails." There were still mysteries that could be unveiled.

The camp at the mouth of Redlands Canyon was not only one of the first prospecting camps, there was another reason that this particular piece of landscape was revered. When some of the ill-fated members of the Death Valley 49er wagon train escaped from the clutches of the deepest trough in North America they came out there. Down and around the startling 90-foot vertical natural rock wall that breeched the whole canyon and formed what came to be known as Manly Falls. (The only time there is water at Manly Falls is when the Heavens open up, spilling millions of gallons from often-violent cloudbursts, into the narrow deep canyon above it.)

From his camp you could see most of Panamint Valley spread out below (I used to tell Harry that the view from his place alone was worth a million dollars). This site was where the first miners in the area had built a gold mill. Some of the old buildings or at least their ghost-like remnants were still standing. These wooden skeletons and crumbling walls were testimony to the adventure and excitement that had taken place here in bygone days. Harry had built his palace in the middle of this old mill, in fact on top of the mill tailings there. His first shelter was a big army tent with a wooden plank floor. Later he expanded this into one big room built around the old tent floor. There was a small bedroom at the far end. The large room served as kitchen, living room and office. There was a nice overhang porch up front and under this same roof there was a cozy little shower room, or stall, a real luxury in this part of the country. Another bonanza was the drip system that he had rigged up to cool the summer breeze. It was a hose strung high up in a row of salt cedar trees he had planted along the driveway west of the building. The hose was perforated so that the water that came via a small pipeline from a spring a mile up the canyon was dripping in the breeze all the time. In the summer Harry would sleep on a cot outside by the tree line.

One time, while prospecting above his camp I found a large quartz boulder that had gold showing here and there. I rolled it an eighth of a mile down the side of the mountain and into the bed of my truck. I dumped it right at the head of his cot and it was there for years, but it kept getting smaller because people kept breaking off pieces.

There were many old workings or claims around then and

the campsite was just one of the many Harry ended up with, one way or another. As it turned out the best one of his mines was the one just above his camp there in Redlands Canyon.

Before World War II, Harry got into a legal battle with a wealthy mine developer over a claim way over near Mojave, California. Harry won not only the claim but also the respect and friendship of his adversary. The money man took a liking to him and when he saw some samples Harry had from Redlands Canyon they formed a partnership.

With a government loan they developed several exploratory tunnels into a large low-grade ore body just above the 90-ft. dry falls there. The falls were a famous landmark that formed a sentinel like-buttress between Redlands Canyon and Panamint Valley. They built a road that climbed up and around the falls and were able to develop a lot of ore. World War II put the kibosh to the operation and the millions of tons excavated during the tunneling formed a big stockpile of complex ore. At that time it was not profitable to mill this ore. When his partner died, his widow gave Harry full rights to the claim.

Harry didn't like to talk to tourists, unlike the typical desert recluse (or story teller like Russell). Harry was more of a doer. He would get up early in the morning and with a steaming cup of coffee laced with a little whiskey (Harry did not booze it up but liked a little beer now and then.) he would sit at his big desk and listen to the news on the radio. After he heard the price of gold on the market report he'd head out to work on whatever had priority for that day. He had named his mine the Southern Homestead Mine after the famous mine in the Black Hills of North Dakota.

We got along all right I think because he respected me as a prospector. He really amazed me as his energy was unbelievable.

There was a story that I had heard going around that there was a secret gold mine a few miles north of his Southern Homestead. The story was that the man that found it had died of cancer a short time back. His doctor, who had gone into partnership with him on the mine, had been killed while on an emergency call. His car battery connection came loose and he got out in the dark to fix it and was struck down by another motorist.

One of the people that had been broadcasting this story was a bartender at the Owl Saloon in an old mining town (Red Mountain, way south on one of the roads that lead to Death Valley) who was showing his patrons a gold-laced bolo tie clip that his late friend, the guy who had found the mine, had given him. Well, this lost gold mine was a hot topic in the booze-fueled town of Ballarat and now that these guys were gone, no one was supposed to know where their diggins' were.

I mentioned this story to Harry one day and he said, "Well I know where it is; it's way up the mountain above the old Cecil R Mine. There is a trail that leads off to the north, if we can find it, that will take us to it. Come on, let's go up there, it's early."

I didn't know what a fireball this guy was then and I had second thoughts about dragging this old man thousands of feet up a nearly vertical hillside on the slim prospect that we might find something on this hot summer day.

We went up there in Harry's green International. And what do you know—it didn't take long before we found a trail above the "Cecil R" and it did head off to the north. Harry stepped around me and took off, and soon he was quite a ways ahead of me. An hour later when we came to the enriched quartz streak running through a granite outcrop, I said, "I thought nobody knew where this was!"

"Well, the bartender told my friend Earl Fox that the doctor had hired an Indian to build a trail for them and Earl figured out somehow where he started and he scouted around until he found it and he told me about it."

I was still breathing hard from trying to catch the old man. There was some nice rock scattered around where they had been digging, specimen ore with green and blue stains that was the usual sign hereabouts that the quartz might be flecked with gold. However, the vein looked too small to gamble on.

"Well, here it is, Emmett, if you feel like doing some exploration sometime let me know."

What I learned that day was not to underestimate Mr. Briggs.

As a side note, years later I did go back there with a helicopter with Ron Burch. We picked up and stashed a lot of the good-looking loose rock in the litter basket. Finally the pilot said, "If you boys pick up anymore of this gold ore we are not going to be able to take off."

Like I said Harry was a doer. He talked me into helping him build a landing field at the Redlands camp. He had drug in an ancient old road-grading machine from somewhere. It must have been vintage 1901. It had to be pulled having no engine of its own. There was no place to sit; the operator had to stand between two large control wheels that would raise and adjust the blade. Harry decided to use a 4x4 dump truck that he had salvaged to pull it with. In order to get enough traction to pull the grader he went about fixing up dual wheels for the front wheels as well as the rear wheels. He also loaded the bed of the truck with boulders. Now he was not a big man and I don't know how he could steer that truck with its heavy load and those ponderous wheels up front. But steer it he did. He dragged me and that grader back and forth, back and forth, hundreds of times down near the road below his camp. If I would have gotten hung up in the wheels and levers on the grader I don't know how long I'd have been tangled up before Harry would have stopped. I thought I should have had a jerk-line tied to him like they used to have on the lead mule on the twenty-mule- team borax wagons. Oh, he would stop every now and then and come back with a bottle of beer for me, "Let's take a vitamin pee break Emmett," he'd say.

We did get a fine landing strip built. And before we had the grader pulled clear away from the runway an airplane buzzed the field and then came right in over the top of our machinery and settled in for a nice landing. The pilot of the plane was Jim Campbell. As luck would have it he would play an important part later on in our further adventures.

As I said, Harry's Southern Homestead Mine turned out to be a good gold mine. I just wish Harry could have seen what it has turned into today.

While Harry was still with us, some friends of his helped him to interest some modern mining companies in the property. They would fly in and bring their geologists and take samples. Then one company decided to do more extensive discovery work and they paid Harry, I believe, $20,000 for an option. They backed out after spending that much and more on development work, building roads and core drilling and so forth. Then another outfit came in and they paid him even more to tie up the mine.

Harry bought a new truck and Ruth and I helped him get a big camper on it. We also took him to a tax expert. He was worried that the IRS government hounds would come after him. The consultant, Mr. Adams, amortized all that he had done over the years and told him not to worry. But worry he did, anyway.

Along this line I'd like to comment that in more than one case we were familiar with, these old-timers could handle poverty just fine, but prosperity wasn't as easy. In fact for several it was not a good thing and often it was their undoing. I do remember a scene that took place in the big room at the Redlands Canyon camp soon after Harry had started to get some big payments. Carl Ruona and I were sitting there and Harry was at his big desk, grumbling over the paperwork in front of him. Carl said, "You know, Harry, dat money is no dammed good for you." What the hell do you mean, Carl?" Harry scoffed back at him. "Vell, look at you. You used to be happy. Now you wring your hands and worry too much."

One tax consultant wasn't enough. There was another $40,000 payment in the wind. So this old man drives his big truck all the way to Bishop, California to talk to another taxman. Then back to the Panamints the same day, over 250 miles. Instead of going to his camp he drove up high into the hills (the doctor had told him to avoid high altitude) to visit with Norma and Jim Weston at their camp in Happy Canyon near Ballarat.

Norma and Jim were glad to have Harry visit them at their high camp. They had a few cocktails and then Harry turned in. In the morning the Westons were fixing breakfast and when they went to Harry's camper he wasn't there. They found his body on the trail back from the outhouse.

It would have been nice if we could have buried him at Ballarat, but that wasn't allowed. The service was held in the small cemetery at Trona. It was however a typical western funeral. Harry would have been proud. The grave was dug by some

The Briggs Camp about 1977, taken from a helicopter. The camp now is gone but was located in the middle of the present C. R. Briggs Corporation mine. Photo by author.

Recent picture of the C. R. Briggs Corporation mine at the mouth of Redlands Canyon as it looks today. Photo by Ron McKinley.

of his personal friends. At the graveside ceremony there was a large turnout of local people who felt the loss of this pioneer prospector. After I gave the eulogy we placed his modest casket in the shallow grave and the crowd mingled as we covered him and filled the grave.

I am proud to say that in a big way the ghost of Harry Briggs still lives on in Panamint Valley. Today, halfway between Ballarat and Goler Wash, you will find the most modern gold mine in the whole Death Valley area. Canyon Resources out of Denver, Colorado ended up with Harry's Homestead Mine and they spent around $30,000,000 to develop it. They formed The Briggs Corporation and that company has been shipping gold out through Ballarat for many years.

Harry's brother and sister that were shorted their wages when Harry had gone belly up in the oil business ended up well rewarded by their brother's gold mine in the west.

THE MAN FROM ODESSA

Their relationship seemed to be almost a father and son bond. Even though they were both well advanced in years before they had ever met, it was obvious that these two desert denizens had adjusted into a comfortable symbiotic existence. Leon had a serious heart disorder as the result of an explosion years before so he pretty much hibernated as a caretaker at the Briggs camp. That

Leon Griffin, "the man from Odessa" and author's wife Ruth. Photo by author.

was a great relief for Harry to have someone to be there so he could get away from the camp and not have to worry about all the equipment he had brought in there through the years. Harry would do all the shopping, which included Leon's medication (at least a quart of whiskey a week).

As I heard it, Harry found Leon high in the mountains one snowy day walking along through the scrub pines. I forget why Harry was up there, probably checking on one of his high camps or one of the many claims he had acquired over the years, anyway there was this stocky bearded Texan, hungry and cold, slowly shuffling along the rock-strewn, snow dusted path that had been the road to the great Ratcliff gold mine and mill, in a era past.

In a thick Texas drawl, Leon explained that he had been a successful businessman back in Odessa until he went to jail and after that he had come to California to get away. He had hired on as a caretaker at the old mine camp and the owners had left him and a load of grub high up Pleasant Canyon and promised to be back to resupply him later in the season. Well, the season had come and gone and Leon was out of grub and real disappointed, and as I recall, possibly lost. Going the wrong way.

I liked this old Odessan. He always said what he thought even if it wasn't the popular thing to say, and though he moved and talked slowly his stocky build and weathered features made him look pretty ornery. And even though his disability left him physically weak he could stand his ground verbally, and he always carried a small automatic pistol in his pants pocket.

One day I came by their camp to talk to Harry about some mining. Harry wasn't there but Leon was in a mood to talk and he invited me down to his gray, shabby little old house trailer. "I love fried chicken so come on and I'll fix you the best chicken you ever et."

It was only a short distance downhill from the main shack to the trailer but it took Leon a while to make the trip. What a spot! The rest of the camp was above and behind the house trailer, so the whole beautiful brown desertscape, the south end of Panamint Valley, was spread out below his rickety metal front step. It was one of those perfect days in the desert, almost cool, even with the clear bright sky. The air was still; a quiet time. You could appreciate the magic of the wasteland.

We climbed in; I sat by the small foldout table on a frail metal chair while Leon went to frying us his specialty. I wish I had paid more attention to the way he fixed it. I believe he used a syrup in his gravy or something. He wasn't kidding; it turned out to be the best fried chicken of all my travels.

Through the small window I could see minor dust devils dancing across the bone-dry floor of the lakebed in the valley below us. Our conversation was just general banter until the meal was ready and Leon settled on a chair across from me. The window behind him framed his features, square rugged jaw, wrinkled sun-baked face with a short stubble of gray beard topped off with a full head of curly gray hair. He began to tell me why he had left Odessa.

"I used to own a good business, welding shop, several people worked for me. Ya know that is oil well country down there. There was an old pipeline to an abandoned field; it was big, long and unused. For years I had driven by it. Every time I thought about how it would be ta scrap it out, hell, nobody would care. Well I was wrong, they did care, a lot! I went to jail for quite a spell. My family sold the shop and they disowned me completely. Wouldn't have nothin' to do with me." His eyes filled with tears as he went on to say, "Hell, they won't even write or talk to me now and that's been a long time." He realized he was going down the wrong path and so he turned the conversation around and told me about one of the highlights of his youth. He was soon out of the doldrums as he recalled when he was a big strapping teenager working at the Grand Canyon one summer. "There was these school teachers on vacation, four of them, and they said they needed a guide. Well that wasn't all they needed, I tell you that was some summer. I growed up a lot that summer."

Even after Leon had come to the desert he got into trouble once. I think it was DUI; anyway he spent some time in the slammer. While he was away his Plymouth sedan was parked in the ghost town of Ballarat. Paul Jones and his friends would look after it, and they did. They took the engine out of it and then to get rid of the crude reminder of their stewardship gave the rest of the car to an outfit that was setting up a mining camp a few miles south. They dug a hole with their bulldozer, poked a hole in the car's roof, and buried it as a septic tank. So Leon was afoot when he got back from his vacation. I thought it was an ignoble end to his car.

Leon was the caretaker of the Briggs camp during the time the Manson family were making Death Valley their playground. There were a few times when they came to the Briggs camp and enlisted Leon's help. One dark night some of the boys were coming down the Panamint Valley road with a Hertz rental pickup truck, way overloaded with five fifty-gallon barrels of gasoline. They made a common mistake; in the dark of the night it was easy to turn off the main road at the wrong place. They turned one canyon too soon and went up Coyote Canyon instead of Goler Wash. When they realized their mistake, they tried to turn around in the soft sand and got stuck. A couple of the boys made a long hike back to the Briggs camp and asked Leon to help them. Leon, in his old truck, took them back down to their dilemma and when they got there they wanted him to help get them out of the soft sand. "I ain't going to do nothin'. You guys just roll those barrels out on the sand and then push that truck out of its ruts, turn it around headed back down the road and then put them barrels back in, O.K.?" Leon laughed when he told us about what happened.

Another time Leon probably had a closer call than he realized. Since he had run a welding shop and the "Family" were into fixing dune buggies up like Mad Max desert patrol machines (machine gun mounts and so forth) they invited him up to their hideout up Goler. He said they had Volkswagen parts all over the place. "While I was helping them with the welding I saw this guy Manson doing some sort of a weird, jangly St. Vitus dance, I spoke up and asked the boys, What the hell is wrong with that crazy son-of-a-bitch? They laughed and Manson just slinked away."

It wasn't until later that Leon learned most of the Volkswagens there were stolen and some of the owners were missing.

A LONG WAY DOWN

Clair M. Kunkel was a consulting geological engineer. He was also a great guy and a good friend of Harry Briggs. In 1975 he and I were to share an adventure that would scare the hell out of a reasonable man.

After I had taken the high-grade gold and tungsten ore down from the old Lost Mormon Mine near the top of Manly Peak, we left the mine well stocked. With the help of the helicopter it was well supplied with fuel, food and even metal army cots. Talk about high-class! We even had a generator up there and the tunnel was equipped with a string of electric lights.

Many days spent in the field and hours pouring over records and history books had given me an intimate vision of the Mormon pioneers who had first started to mine on Manly Peak. It was apparent that they were here building trails and mining gold while the folks down in Los Angeles were reading in the newspaper about the Lost Brefogle Mine and the mysteries of Death Valley, dreaming about untouchable treasures. I came to admire the character and strength of these men and women who were out here doing the things that the city folk just dreamed of.

And so it came to pass that I joined the Church of Jesus Christ of Latter-Day Saints (Mormons). I became good friends with my Bishop, Dan Dedricksen, a giant of a man whose family came from Iceland; in fact an ancestor, Thor Dedricksen, helped found a large city in that country. Dan was one of the nicest people you would want to meet. And though he was big and strong he was also agile—as a youth he had worked on the railroad as a gandy dancer (the men with hammers that drive the heavy spikes that hold the rails down).

It was wintertime when Dan and Clair and I decided to climb Manly Peak, up to the Mormon Mine. Dan wanted to see the mine and Clair and I had a special agenda we were going to pursue as well.

We arrived at Russell's camp, via Goler Wash, in the afternoon. We were soon packed up and headed up the mountain. Dan's

4-WD car was left at Russell's. It was with some concern that we left the vehicle there with no one to look after it. Anyway, we started hiking up the pack trail to the first ridge, glancing back occasionally to see the rustic encampment disappear.

We were on our way clear to the top of the mountain. I wanted to show Dan an outcrop of fluorescent ore that was beside the large granite boulders that crowned the peak before we went on to the mine. We

Bishop Dan Dedricksen, the author's Bishop, friend and fellow prospector.

came to the snow level at 6,000 feet. At the top, even though there was a foot of snow, we found the spot we were looking for just before dark. While we prowled about, the sky was getting cloudy and there was fresh wind coming up. After the sun faded, the black light that we had with us lit up the outcrop of specimen ore. It looked like a small cluster of stars. Dan loaded his pack with the best samples he could find and then the three of us headed north, crunching through the freezing snow.

I couldn't resist saying, "Hey, what if we can't find the mine portal in the dark. It looks like it's going to snow some more soon. I hope we don't get stuck out in the elements at this altitude."

They didn't say much, so I couldn't tell if I had them worried or not. I led them over the north buttress and down the steep face and soon we were at the mine portal. As luck would have it we ended up with only one weak flashlight between us, but we soon found our way around and got the power plant fired up and the lights on.

We cooked dinner on a camp stove set up at the mine landing. A plastic bottle half full of water that wasn't close enough to the fire froze solid. Outside it was getting colder, but in the mine it was quite comfortable. Dan, a little claustrophobic, wasn't thrilled about being inside the mountain but the weather helped him to accept holing up there. He did however insist on having the bunk nearest the portal.

As we enjoyed the shelter of the old Mormon diggings, I told Dan and Clair the story about how Russell had tried to talk me out of looking for this mine. Russell had warned me that the mysterious Mormons would get me if they found out I was trying to find their concealed mine. When I finished the tale, Bishop Dan laughed as he declared, "Hey, Russell was sort of a prophet wasn't he?"

"What do you mean?" I asked.

"Well, we did get you, didn't we!"

As our camp talk continued, Clair and I formulated the plan for the next day's operations. He and I were going to make our way down the west face of the mountain to another hidden gold mine— maybe!

Don Landells had called me before we made this trip, and he told me that while he was flying, with a couple of surveyors in his helicopter over the west side of the peak, he remembered I had told him the story, a local legend, about a secret camp that was supposed to be located high up on that side of the mountain. Actually, I had told him only part of the story, not mentioning that the camp was associated with a high-grade pocket of gold and quartz. I only asked him to look for that camp if he got over that way.

When I shared that tale with Don, I did not have much faith in it. I told him that the landmarks that were supposed to mark the camp, a spring and a large willow tree, should have been easy to spot. Why was this place with a little stone house, if it really existed, supposed to be lost? But I did, off chance, mention the camp to Don.

One of the reasons I was curious about this mystery was because I did know of some rich specimen ore that had been found beside a pack trail that may have come from that camp. In fact, I

Don Landells landing at Briggs Camp. Panamint Valley in the background.
Photo by author.

myself had found some rich gold ore that looked as if it had
spilled from a burro pack on the same trail. This was in a canyon
that might have been used as one way to get up on that side of the
mountain where the little stone cabin was supposed to have been
located.

As I said, I was not the only one to find some of this enriched ore. An old prospector, who had been in that country many
years before with Carl Mengel, stopped by my house one day
after he had read a newspaper article about me and my doins' in
the Butte Valley area. He wanted to share with my wife, Ruth,
and me some of his experiences in that country back in the 1930s.
Now, as he talked, he gave me some important history. Apparently, he did not know anything about the stone cabin story that I
would later tell Don Landells, so on this score we were surprised
when he told us, "One day when Carl Mengel and I were headed
out Redlands Canyon with our pack train, going to Ballarat for
supplies, we came upon quite a bit of rich gold ore that had been
spilled at a spot along the trail. It was so good that we packed it
up and turned around and hurried back to our camp in Butte Val-

ley to crush and pan it. By God, it gave us a new little grubstake, around two hundred, if I remember right." The ore he described matched what I had found.

There was another legend that I had heard that our visitor did not know about. It was about a patient in the Los Angeles General Hospital suffering from extreme exposure that told a nurse on his death bed that he had come out of the Panamint Mountains with burros loaded with rich ore and that he had lost most of it after his burro died from a snake bite. He was supposed to have validated his story by bequeathing some remaining gold to her. He died trying to tell her where he stashed the rest of his treasure after his pack animals gave out. This man's account in detail seemed to point to the little stone camp as the spot where he was supposed to have spent a season milling out gold, using only a cast-iron mortar and pestle attached to a spring-like limb of the willow tree. Until Don Landells' phone call, none of us knew of any sign of a willow tree on that side of the mountain.

When Don called me, I heard him say, "Emmett, remember that spot you wanted me to look for on the west side? The other day I found it!"

Don was one of those people who have been blessed with special visual perception. Some people can see things that are invisible to most of us. For example, while climbing with a fellow who was colorblind, I was startled by the fact that he noticed things I had missed, even though I had made that same trip several times.

Don reported, "The willow tree and the camp have been burned and that was why it did not stand out. It was a tight spot to land in. The wash below the stonewalls of the shelter was very narrow.

"I want to apologize. We, the surveyors and I, were excited and as I was landing we agreed to share one and all, but I had to stay with the bird as the engine idled down. The others raced to the ruins and started grabbing everything they could. One of them found a beautiful small whiskey barrel and the other guy found a cast-iron mortar. I'm sorry, some of the artifacts they got would have meant something to you."

Don Landells helicopter, piloted by Mike Donavan, on the right and the bare floor and stone walls of the mine camp are on the left. Photo by author.

So there in the old Mormon mine tunnel that night, Clair and I were planning our assault. We were going to see if we could find the spot where Don landed, while Dan was going down the east side. He was going back the same way we came up.

This was the day before Thanksgiving. We all planned to meet the evening of the next day with Clair's wife, Marie, at the Briggs Camp in Panamint Valley. She came down with Clair from Lone Pine, and we were going to have a big Thanksgiving feast. Dan said he would make his way out through the snow with his heavy backpack down to Russell's and get the car. He would go back down Goler Wash and around to Briggs's camp.

He planned to look for Clair and me along the Panamint Valley road in the late afternoon.

We all were awake at first light. Framed by the tunnel opening, the gray sky looked like a soiled curtain. In a hurry to get going we did not take much time for breakfast.

It would be an easy trip for Clair and me. We were old hands at this. Clair was about 70 but he had hiked in the mountains all his life. He was in great shape, tall and strong. We planned on dropping rapidly down the west side. With the field glasses we had borrowed from Dan, we would scour the landscape. Now that we knew that the secret camp was real, we were confident that we could find it. We would be descending over 4,000 feet but the linear distance was well within our range.

What we were worried about was Dan. He would be descending alone through a rugged landscape that he was totally unfamiliar with and part of his trek would be in the snow. Of course there was the heavy backpack too. We counseled him carefully on how to find the camp where his car was. We talked to him seriously about the many hazards he would encounter in Goler Wash. It was even mentioned that there might still be some Manson followers in that part of the badlands.

With some trepidation and guilt, I shook his hand and watched as he trudged off into the snow, a lonely figure with a heavy burden. He seemed to sink out of sight as I assuaged myself with the idea that I had great confidence in him. In retrospect, I think that Clair and I wouldn't have been so inclined to divide our party had we not been so anxious to tackle the challenge that was beckoning us just over the horizon.

We watched until Dan disappeared completely. I said, "Good Luck, Dan." We gathered our gear. We were traveling light to make good time. Our only food was half of a large bag of M&M candies. We would save our appetites for the big dinner at the Briggs camp. We had one GI canteen of water. It was cold, so we would not need much. I brought along a sleeping bag that had been in the mine just because I wanted to take it home for one of the kids. We marched off confidently. I had just a light pack and Clair did not have any.

We headed into a small bowl-like valley nestled on the west side of the top of the mountain. The snow there was waist-deep in several places. We were attracted toward a peculiar arrangement of large boulders protruding out of the snowfield. Soon we could see there was a natural shelter large enough for four or five people. "Let's check it out, it might be a good refuge in an emergency," Clair said.

Surprise! Inside we found the remnants of an old camp, several artifacts, dishes, pans and other camp gear. We laughed as we congratulated ourselves on being at least as wise as some of the old sourdoughs of the past.

When we came to the western lip of the little valley we could see Panamint Valley spread out before us, thousands of feet below—a grand sight. Breathtaking for more than one reason, our intended path would be almost vertical in some places. We were at the closed end of what might be called a box canyon. Canyon, hell, it was steep enough to be called a chute! I thought if we kept on the way we were going we would be funneled into a crack-like geological formation that descended quickly to the floor of Panamint Valley.

Making our way out onto the face even further we could now see most of this exposure. We stopped at some boulders where we had good footing, and now being below the snow, we stopped to scan the area to locate the remnants of the rock shelter we were hoping to find. Clair searched with the glasses first and then said, "No." and handed them to me. The field glasses were real good ones and at first I didn't see anything interesting—then, as a wide spot in the sand wash in the very floor of the rocky defile presented itself to me, I shouted, "Look, there are two parallel straight lines in the sand there!" Handing the glasses to Clair and pointing, I said, "That must be where the helicopter landed." "Yes, Emmett—and I see the rock walls in the shadows above the sand bar!"

We were excited and I hardly noticed the steep terrain on the way down. Yes, it was the legendary site. Furthermore, when we got to it, there were many things still scattered about—remnants of this once cozy shelter. We found the damnedest mousetrap I had ever seen: round and with a place for bait in the middle, it could trap six mice, each one with its own gate. There were many things the fire had not destroyed. I had the opportunity to come back later and find the hidden spring. That day though, one exciting thing we did find that the boys in the helicopter missed was the pestle for the mortar they had taken. For us the outstanding thing about this artifact was that it was fastened into a piece of pipe where it had been attached to a tree limb, thereby lending credence to the story about the prospector and his gold.

Clair felt bad when he broke it taking it out of the pipe. We didn't stay long. We had some way to go yet and it was already after noon. We stopped just long enough to look around, eat our M&Ms and drink some water.

I did have in my pack some climbing rope, four homemade pitons, a light rock hammer and two pair of light cotton gloves. Unfortunately we decided to take the direct route, going right down the crack in the mountainside.

The first part was a cakewalk—a smooth gravel floor with majestic sheer rock walls on either side of us reaching for the clear sky above. It was still light, scattered clouds, but the defile we were in twisted and turned and half the time we were in the shadows. The colors were majestic.

We wondered how Dan had made out and if he would be able to meet us. We had told him that if he didn't make it to Briggs' camp, we would come looking for him with a rescue party.

Then the floor of the wash disappeared suddenly. We came to a dry waterfall, a shear rock face that dropped over twenty feet straight down.

We prided ourselves on our luck and having the equipment that we had. After we hammered in a piton and with our fifty-foot rope doubled through the fastener, we rappelled down, pulled the rope through the ring on the piton, coiled it up and marched on. The steady crunch of the gravel was encouraging and we were making good time.

The next shear drop-off was a little higher. This time the doubled rope was not quite long enough. Clair dropped the last few feet, and when I came down, I pulled the rope with me as I slid down to the gravel. I was beginning to sweat and I don't think it was because we were at a lower altitude. The shadows were blending and the colors were less vivid. The next two dry falls weren't much shorter.

Just when we were beginning to think we would get out of this trap, we came to a drop that was over seventy feet. Even if we had any more pitons, even going single strand with our rope, it would have been impossible to have successfully lowered ourselves down this glass-like face.

So there we were, virtually trapped in a rock dungeon we had lowered ourselves into. Now what to do? We tried to climb back up where we had come down, but without any pitons, the slick granite rebuffed our best efforts. Now the light was fading fast. Examining both the north wall and the south wall, the north side seemed more scalable, and it was Clair's notion that if we could gain a ridge of the mountain that way and make it one canyon over, we might locate an old miner's trail that would guide us right into Briggs's camp. As it was, even if we got out to the alluvium anywhere near where we were now, it would be difficult to meet anyone in the dark.

So we started up, freehand rock climbing. If we had known what was ahead of us, we might have been tempted to give up right then and wait for the remote chance of being rescued— somehow. What comes to mind is the saying; "Men often choose death over humiliation."

The air was cooling down as it does in the desert that time of year. Suddenly, the chill came like a curtain with the darkness. The climbing was so exhausting that even as cool as it was we were dehydrating. Our meager depleted canteen of water wasn't going to do much for us.

We were still climbing at a steep angle. As it became dark, it was more nerve-wracking. We could not see below or above us very far, and as we climbed we could hear the rocks we dislodged falling, striking, falling, striking again over and over, falling hundreds of feet. We were tired and quite worried—no belay or safety line if we slipped. What we would have given for a radio! What about Dan? What about our families? We had intended to head home after dinner.

About nine o'clock, we came to a bit of a ledge. It still had quite a slope to it but if we positioned our bodies at right angles to the lip we were able to rest. "We have to stop here for a while. We are tired and if we keep going we are going to make a mistake," Clair said. I knew he was right. I rolled out the sleeping bag where we could both lie on it. We each had an extra pair of socks, and we took off our boots and put on dry socks so that our feet would not start to freeze. Clair lay back, and in moments he was snoring.

I wondered if this old man was going to have a heart attack or something. Good Lord, what have I got us into? As I lay there listening to his steady breathing, the evening chill soaked in, and soon I was shivering. I had to do something. I got up as gently as I could and when clear of the bag, laid my part of it over him. In my stocking feet, I worked around the ledge till there were some protrusions between us. There was enough light to find a little brush. Still shaking badly, I crumpled up a pile of it and started a fire. It was just a small fire, but it was enough to stop my shakes. There was a barrel cactus growing out of the ledge to one side of me. With the rock hammer, I chopped into it, digging out pieces of the pulp and putting them in my large checkered bandana, I twisted it up like a tourniquet and dripped the juice into my mouth.

In about forty-five minutes I woke Clair, "Do you feel like going on? I think we need to reach the ridge and get out of the wind, O.K.?" He nodded, and we put on our boots. It was near midnight before we gained the top of the slope, and later we were to find we had climbed almost 1,800 feet almost vertically since we had left the canyon. It was nice to get behind the big rocks and sit for a while. There was enough moonlight by then so we could have a vague idea of where we were.

What we saw was another discouragement. In order to get to the ridge where we might find the trail down to Briggs' camp, we would have to go back, way around to the east or cross another canyon ahead of us. I told Clair, "To get to that ridge it looks like it would take us all night, and I don't have that much steam left." Clair said, "That's what it looks like to me, too. I'm really thirsty now. Do we have any water left?" I gave him our canteen. There wasn't but a small amount left. After he had a drink and passed it back to me, he asked, "Please save some. We're not going to get off the mountain tonight. I have dentures and in the morning I'll gag if I don't have any water. I think we should drop down into the canyon ahead of us while we have moonlight and see if we can find any water."

I was desperate to quench my thirst. Our arduous climb had left me parched; my throat was dry and my voice cracked. I supposed Clair was just as bad off. It was a relief not to be climbing hand-over-hand any longer. The slope into the canyon was not very steep and as we walked around and through boulder fields, we searched with our hands in the shadows, exploring any flat rocks that may have caught rainwater. It was cold enough that we were not worried about any rattlesnakes and to hell with the scorpions.

Down we went, enjoying the better terrain even if we could feel the fatigue and dehydration enveloping us like a fever. I could not find any moisture at all and finally when the moonlight disappeared, we were in a narrow draw. Clair said, "It's about 3:00 A.M. and it's too dark to travel. Let's rest till the sun comes up a bit." I was beat and that was the best idea I had heard all night. "Yes, let's stop right here." Where we were was solid rock, and if there was any cloudburst up-canyon from us, we would be drowned, but we rolled out the sleeping bag to pad our stone bed and, like before, Clair was instantly asleep. I lay there sure that I couldn't sleep, knowing that I would soon start shivering when the coolness soaked in. I thought of Dan and hoped he had gotten help, and I was wondering about our families; what would Ruth think when I didn't show up.

There is a book about Death Valley's victims and surprisingly in most cases they turned out not to be the greenhorns that made some fatal mistake, instead it was often some old-timer that had forgotten to have enough respect for the harsh desert landscape. Well, it wasn't hard to imagine Clair and myself in that light.

I guess I was too tired to shiver and I fell into a deep sleep. The next thing I knew, Clair was shaking me awake, and he said in a hoarse voice, "Come on, wake up. It's light enough to get going. Where's the canteen?"

After Clair wet his parched throat, he offered me the last swallow. "No, go ahead, Clair. I had some last night. While you were on the ledge I found a barrel cactus. It helped a little."

"I wish we could find one today," he said. I knew that the wash we were in was often scoured by summer rains but there would be little chance of that today. But as I sat up and my eyes adjusted to the gray dawn, low and behold, there, not three feet from him stood a very large cactus. It afforded us some immediate relief.

We found that we were headed down another narrow, steep draw and were amazed to see how high we still were above Panamint Valley. Stunned might have been more appropriate! This time we decided to leave the gash in the mountainside if it looked like we were going to end up like yesterday. On the face we would have better going even if it were very steep.

Before we left the wash, we came to a place where a flat shelf of rock had captured a small puddle of water. Our joy was modified when we found that under the thin layer of precious water there was a layer of mountain sheep droppings. We were so thirsty that this did not deter us and we siphoned off the liquid gently with our lips. "Even if I get sick, it will take a while and maybe we will be off the mountain by then," I said.

Not long after that bonanza, we found a boulder with a crack in it that had trapped some more water. The only problem was that the opening, wide at the top, narrowed down to where we could not reach the water. I remembered, as a child, reading a book of Aesop's Fables. In it one story was about a crow faced with the same kind of problem. I used his solution for our dilemma. We jammed the canteen down into the crack as far as we could. Then gathering small pebbles from the gravel pan we fed them into the crack until the water level came up high enough to fill the canteen. We had a good drink and left with a whole canteen full of water—what a treasure!

Out on the face of the mountain we made good time climbing and in places glissading down. It was steep enough that we were in constant danger until we got near the base. Then, just above the alluvium, we came across an old Indian trail that paralleled the valley below and headed in the direction of Briggs' camp. We celebrated this good fortune by consuming half of our remaining water. We still had a long way to go, however. With the smooth trail, new adrenaline flooded through our fatigued legs. We practically flew the rest of the way.

It was about 9:00 A.M. when we came around a large outcrop and the camp was in sight not far below us and, as soon as we were close enough, we hailed the camp. Surprise! Only Marie was there. Clair and I shuffled into the building where she was and attacked the food that she hastily set out.

Clair Kunkel on left, author on right in front of B3 heliocopter. Photo by author.

Between bites, we asked anxiously if Dan had made it and why was she was the only one in camp. She said, "Bishop Dan got back without any problems—he and some guys from the camp have been frantically trying to find out what happened to you two! We had decided that one of you broke a leg or something and they expected the other one of you to turn up. They have been back and forth between here and Russell's two or three times. They thought that the survivor might have returned to that camp."

I told her, "I need some way to get a message out to my family, and Dan's. They expected us back before now."

Marie, chuckled, "We already got in touch."

"Oh no, I'm never going to live this down."

"Hey, we covered your butt this time."

"How's that?

"Using a CB radio here, we were able to raise someone in Trona and we got them to make a phone call to your wife. All they told her was that you guys were held up and would be late. They asked her to relay the message to Dan's people. I am sure glad you showed up. What the devil happened to you? We were just about to revise our message and call in Mountain Rescue from Trona. You sure caused a lot of excitement here."

While telling her our story I hoped she would feel sorry for us in our wasted condition and not be too ready to shame us for our misguided directions. She was quite gracious.

Dan and his companions soon pulled in. Their relief seemed stronger than any other emotion— fortunately.

As I said, I did return to that secret ruins more than once, but you can bet that I was equipped with some great topographical maps and adequate equipment and plenty of water. I found a better route, that's for sure. Once I used a helicopter to make a spectacular visit there. The contrast was startling; the trip, each way, took less than ten minutes.

On my desk top there is a welded-together, cast-iron pestle.

BEYOND THIS POINT
THERE BE DRAGONS

Russell had a dramatic story to tell about a great brown lizard with green blades down its back, like a dinosaur. It came out of the dark brown pile of granite boulders that covered the south side of the canyon where his cabin was. He and a friend were sitting in the shade in front of the camp, one afternoon, summer sun at a high angle. This thing stretched itself right in Russell's driveway. It was so big, over ten feet long.

So far as I know no one else ever saw this monster. This happened I believe at Russell's camp, way back when he and his friend were making "white lightning" in a still that was hidden under the floor of a tent that had a trap door.

He always knew that creature was still around somewhere and he would caution me to be on the lookout for it.

I really never expected to meet *Flintstone's* Barney Rubble's pet but thru the years I had several encounters with various wild creatures in that part of the desert. Some of these

Russell's camp, showing a building over the site of where the whiskey tent was located. Photo by Ron McKinley.

small adventures might seem almost as hard to believe, with or without "White Lightning."

The road down Panamint Valley was shimmering hot and the three vehicles that were hitched all together left a contrail of smoke like dust as far as I could see behind me. It was so hot the blaze of the sun seemed almost to melt the rocks. I know that only "mad dogs and Englishmen go out in the noonday sun." Prospectors are an exception. I had some money coming if I could deliver some of the blue-green marble-like rock out of Goler Wash. My outfit was a truck and trailer with a Jeep on behind. There was no way that the truck could make it up Goler Wash, but working alone I could blast the picture rock down from the wall of the canyon, break it up with a sledge hammer and tote it down to the truck and trailer half-a-ton at a time.

I wasn't very far from where the road turned up the wash when the cylinder-head temperature went off scale. The dust settled and the sereneness of the desert took over. It was so peaceful. The metallic screech of the truck door opening seemed to call out like a banshee. With the hood up and the water can ready it would still be a while before the engine cooled enough to take off the radiator cap.

Standing in the shade of the truck cab sweating profusely I heard a delicate clicking sound, and as I turned toward it I was startled to see a medium-sized blackbird hopping along the edge of the road toward me. He stopped in the shade of the front wheel and looked at me.

"What the hell's a matter, too hot to fly?"

There was a GI canteen cup on the seat and I filled it with water, put it on the ground and stepped back. "I'll bet you're thirsty."

The bird hopped up to the cup, but instead of drinking it hopped into the cup, using it as an improvised birdbath. After the radiator was taken care of the bird had disappeared, leaving the metal cup almost empty and water splashed all around it.

On the road again, "There is no way anyone would believe that."

THE COOL RABBIT

Midsummer it was 110 degrees on the valley floor and this time I was driving a white 1962 Ford Econoline Van—virtually a tin box with an engine in the middle. I loved it. It was so light that even with a small six-cylinder engine it had a great power-to-weight ratio and could go some places that a 4 x 4 couldn't. It rode a lot better than a Jeep. One thing it did not have was an air conditioner. I had driven up the paved east side road to the Death Valley Monument Headquarters to turn in some paperwork on my claims and contribute some rock samples from our mine to their geologist for the Monument's specimen display. So on the way back to my camp, retracing my way along the valley floor, sometimes below sea level the heat was oppressive and my only relief was placing my big red bandana on my head and pouring water over it. The camp at the aluminum cabin was over 5,000 feet in elevation and I was quite anxious to get up there out of the caldron and get some relief from the heat. To my sweat-streaked surprise there was an atmospheric inversion layer that day and it

View of the author's aluminum cabin in Woods Canyon. Photo by Ron McKinley.

was still 110 degrees at the cabin. Now I was thankful for my cabin roof water collection system; there was a lot of water in the four hundred gallon tank. In the rocky crag down hill from the tank, on a narrow strip of sand, I had a pallet that served as a shower platform. In no time I had a garden hose strung out with a spray nozzle. I could not get out of my clothes fast enough.

Then, as I marveled at the cooling effect, almost chilling, of the water spray, not fifteen feet away I noticed a cottontail rabbit. It seemed to be transfixed watching me wasting such a precious commodity. I had never even seen a cottontail at the cabin before and for it to expose itself to a strange human animal was, I thought, a desperate miracle of some kind (I have since learned at a desert symposium that every year in hot dry weather the majority of the rabbit population in the Great Basin perish).

This reminded me of the blackbird happening, but this time I didn't talk to the bunny, I don't know why. It might have been I couldn't imagine any rabbit verbs, but everyone knows that birds talk.

Close by there was a shiny tin pie plate. Without making any sudden moves I placed the tin full of water on the pallet. I retreated and waited. Brer rabbit cautiously hopped up onto the boards, over to the tin, and then he too, like the bird, stepped into the middle of the water. He squatted there for several minutes. I felt like this was the best thing I had done all day.

MOUNTAIN SHEEP

The wild mountain sheep in the Panamints are one of the most elusive of all the creatures that live there. You can be around the hills, up and down the deep craggy canyons and visit dozens of remote springs for years and never catch glimpse of these phantom-like animals. They usually stay to the high country and they can glide up vertically impossible terrain as if they are not affected by gravity.

One summer Harry Briggs said, "Some mountain sheep are starting to come to my high camp." His Banta Camp was high up in South Park Canyon. It was Harry's habit, customary with most of the old-timers in the summer when the weather really started warming up, to move to a camp high up out of the valley, and of course in the winter to migrate to the warmer elevations. I didn't think much about his mountain sheep claim, since there was a spring a short distance up the wash from the Banta Camp. And since it was quiet and peaceful with Harry up there alone he might be able to see one now and then. It was likely that they would become accustomed to his company. "Harry, you ought to take a picture of them."

Russell used to tell that when he first started prospecting in the Butte Valley area some Indians were still living there. And once when he and his partner ran low on supplies that the Indians told him they could get a mountain sheep for meat if they would follow instructions. They were not to smoke or chew tobacco and not to wear clothes that had been around anyone who did. They were to go down Redlands Canyon to the spring (beyond the Jeep trail half a mile) the night before and hide under an overhang that formed sort of a cave in the south wall of the canyon, a little above the dense growth of willows. They were to not build a fire. If they were lucky and quiet early in the morning at first light they might get a shot at a wild sheep when they came down to the spring.

He said, "We did as they told us but in the morning instead we heard this strange crunching sound. You know how twisty the canyon is there, something strange was coming up the canyon from around the bend. Crunch, crunch, crunch! We looked at each other and didn't know what to do. We were petrified, forgot we had the gun. When up the wash came five or six gray-bearded old men, bent over walking with long walking sticks. We stammered out, 'HELLO!' It turned out that they were a group of Mormon elders who were on their way to visit the camp of their youth in Woods Canyon." Russell didn't get any sheep for his larder that day.

Well, back to the Banta Camp. This camp in the 1930s had been a working and profitable mill site for the Suitcase Mine. The mine was located a short distance down South Park Canyon from the mill. The camp had a shop building and mining machinery. The main building was a comfortable weathered board shack with a large open living room and kitchen. By the front door, facing east, there was a narrow little wooden porch, just a bit larger than the old rusty car seat springs there leaning against the building.

Harry had worked doing assessment work on the claims for the owners and the war came and the road washed out. Harry put the road back in later and he ended up with the property and he had good luck mining some gold there.

I was visiting Harry; he had been going up to check on things and I rode up to the camp with him. We had sandwiches and beans for lunch in the main building and were carrying on a lively discussion. Since Harry was hard of hearing I was speaking loudly. It was a nice bright sunny day. After Harry had acquired the camp he developed a small spring north of the cabin and piped water in that supported a nice devils grass lawn beyond the porch. He had a fence around it to keep the burros away. After eating I walked out to the porch and lay on the springs. We kept on talking, with Harry inside. I was almost shouting.

Something caught my eye. On the light brown barren slope uphill from the fence there was a trail with six mountain sheep coming down toward the building. I was excited, but I decided not to change my tone of voice or make any sudden moves. The sheep bunched up on the other side of the barrier and then two of them jumped over the wire and started grazing on Harry's grass. I kept on talking. The sheep came closer and closer. It was spooky, their eyes were yellow and they were close enough I could have touched them. A lot of grass was sticking out from under the boards of the old porch and two of the brave creatures were yanking and pulling at it.

Harry finally sauntered out my way and he almost let out a whoop when he saw my company, "See, see! I told ya they were hanging around here. Now maybe someone will believe me, keep talking while I get my camera."

After the sheep left, Harry told me about one time he was taking a nap on an old army cot set out in the middle of his lawn. When he woke up it took his eyes a while to focus and as he sat up he noticed there was a big cow patty right where he was going to put his feet down. "I thought, boy that is strange— then I realized that it was not a cow pile, but a big coiled rattlesnake."

BURROS

Then there was a close encounter with a much bigger denizen of the badlands. Now at that time there were hundreds of burros living on the playas and valleys around Butte Valley. And I had amused myself experimenting to see if I could walk into a grazing herd. The burro makes a blowing, wet-lip sound as sort of a friendly greeting among themselves. By imitating their crude sound and by walking very slowly, waiting a minute between each step, I could make my way amongst them.

Author and his children, left to right, Gerald, Lynn, Dad and Glen, riding friendlier wild burros in Warm Springs Canyon. Photo by Ruth Harder.

The old wranglers that came up to hunt burros were an interesting bunch themselves. One of these colorful characters was the typical rough-cut cowboy. I met him once deep into the badlands, all alone on a good-looking horse. I remember he was old and wrinkled with his beat-up, stained Stetson tilted back and he had a GI canteen hanging from the worn saddle horn on a bent wire coat hanger. He was famous down at ranger headquarters.

Ruth Harder with wild burros at Russell's camp.
Photo by author.

They said that he was in the office one time and we asked him how dangerous the wild burros were. He said, "Well they can be pretty ornery, sometimes they kick you (he demonstrated by kicking the closest ranger in the leg) and they bite (he grabbed the same ranger and jerked him around by the arm violently). The trick is to pick up a couple of rocks and if he comes after you throw one of the rocks at it, usually he will veer away—but don't throw the other rock, cause if he gets a hold of you, he'll hang on like a Gila monster, and he won't let go. You have to hit him between the eyes." And he swung, with an imaginary rock at the ranger who jumped out of the way just in time.

When I was out in the wild herd I kept my arms folded and I had a six-shooter in my right hand, just in case. Now and then a jack would snort and lay his ears back and then trot away a short distance.

One day I had been working late at the mine in Woods Canyon and towards sunset I decided to hike down Redlands to Harry's place. If I hurried I'd make it before dark. It was very picturesque in the canyon, long light and shadows—the colors were rich and

the steep walls gave a special atmosphere to the trip. I was step-
ping out briskly and the sound of my feet on the gravel floor
heralded my presence.

The three burros were just as surprised as I was. I suppose
they expected one of their own. They were a jack and two jennies
and they raced on ahead of me down the wash out of sight. A
short time later I came around a bend and caught up with them,
again they trotted on ahead of me but this time the big jack hung
back a ways. I was traveling light, only carrying a prospector's
rock hammer (the most important tool of all). The third time I
caught up with them the jack had "had it" with me. I came around
the corner and the jennies were way ahead but the jack was standing in the middle of a wide place in the narrow wash, legs spread,
ears back and he let out one of those ear-shattering "HEE–HAWS"
and then he pawed the gravel with his hoof. I didn't have time to
find two hand rocks as the old wrangler had instructed. Standing

*Author with wild burros vistiting Russell's camp. Photo by Ruth
Harder.*

at attention with the prospect pick in my sweaty hand, my arms folded across my chest I tried to look formidable. He wasn't fooling; he put his head down and lunged straight at me. It all happened very fast and just as he was about to run me down he veered sharply to my right. Skidding to a stop on a splay of coarse gravel, he took up a loud bellowing stance opposite me against the wall of the wash. I swallowed hard and tried to walk away with a confident superior posture. He kept vocalizing his complaint but held his ground. The jennies let me pass them at another wide spot.

The windows at the camp were aglow with lantern light when I got there.

EAGLES, RATTLESNAKES & MOUNTAIN LIONS

There were several other times when the wildlife and I shared some scary moments, not the least of which was when I had a close call with a couple of rattlesnakes that struck at me (Russell had assured me that I would not find any rattlesnakes at high altitude—but he forgot to tell the snakes). Or the mountain lion that would make nocturnal visits to my tent camp at the 7,000-foot level (and my camp was on its regular hunting path). The lion was my hazard on top of the mountain and I was cautious that I might climb in amongst the house-size boulders to stumble upon a lioness and her cubs. We stayed out of each other's way but on occasion the cat would call at me from across a far slope.

There were two big eagles that kept track of me, coming by the diggins twice a day, early in the morning and mid-afternoon. Their loud screech was a welcome break in the mountain stillness.

Gerald and Ruth Harder examine a rattlesnake at Russell's camp. Photo by author.

WILD HORSE

Then there was the time a wild horse crossed paths with me. The sky was clear and the weather was mild for a fall day and things were all quiet at Russell's Camp. There were no cars in the sun-bleached decomposed-granite parking area. It was before noon when I pulled in with my Green GMC van. I had not yet bought the aluminum cabin camp but I was going down to check it out and stopped by to check on Russell on the way.

Russell and I were in his kitchen shack extension. We were talking quietly at the round oilcloth-covered table when his old dog, just outside the door, woke up with a start and let us know someone was coming. Almost at the same time a tall trim figure with a full white beard and a bushy head of pure white hair, burst into the kitchen. The screen door slammed behind him. With his battered brown felt hat in his hand and without stopping he bent over the sink and turned on the spigot. Obviously he was very thirsty. He was dressed in blue denims that weren't too old.

This was Ballarat Bob and he said, "I have come up from the Barker Camp and I've heard that my gray horse has been seen up here in Butte Valley."

There had been some talk about some cowboys up from the city on two or three weekends trying to run down a horse in Striped Butte Valley, but nothing had been said about Bob or his horse. This was the first time I had seen him. I was impressed that he was in good shape to have hustled afoot seven miles to Russell's and I thought he was a bit wild to travel like that without a canteen.

After Russ had introduced us, I thought I might do a good deed and help this guy find his horse.

"Let's take my Green Machine out there and drive around the Butte and see what we can find. Looks like it might be all right for you to sit a spell." He readily agreed and we backed out of the gravel and started down the dirt track right away. We were slowly driving past the Butte headed for Redlands Canyon when Bob shouted, "Stop, he crossed the road here." I thought this guy is good. Sure enough the tracks of a shod horse were there at right angles to the road.

"Ya got any rope?"

"Yes, I'll get it." I ran around to the back of the truck opened the tall-windowed van doors, and handed him a medium coil of rope. We headed out following the tracks over a couple of rises and there was the horse. A bay horse! I must have been mistaken—I thought Bob had said his horse was gray.

"There it is, Emmett! I have heard that a man can run a horse down."

He led out stalking the animal. The horse trotted ahead of him. The horse was headed west on out the canyon and so I went back to the truck and drove down the road ahead of them. In a little over a mile the canyon pitched downhill toward Panamint Valley and narrowed way down. At a spot that was not fifteen feet across I pulled up. There and with the back doors open like two wings, the Green Machine almost blocked the way. It wasn't long before here came the horse, straight on. Hollering and waving my arms did not faze him; he rose up on his hind legs, pawed the air, whinnied and snorted, and went right by me and my truck. I might add that horse was mighty tall when he sliced the air near my head—not that I was frightened or anything.

It looked like we had lost the game as Ol' Streak there was beyond me and headed towards Redlands Spring. The wash became too steep and rocky to drive as far as the spring. Well, he wanted to run, so jumping back in the Green Machine the chase was on, Streak trotting vigorously ahead and me pacing him. But, surprise! He suddenly turned left up Woods Canyon. I knew it ended a mile ahead. I had been up this box canyon with Russell once before and there was an aluminum cabin there that had been built by Sid Waley and his wife (this was where I had been headed before Bob showed up at Russell's). It was hard to figure why the horse went that way. My guess was he didn't know about the spring. Streak seemed to have run far enough. When the Green Machine stopped, he stopped a couple of hundred feet ahead. It was still a ways to the end of Woods Canyon but maybe Bob could catch up here.

Old Streak might be thirsty. The only thing in the van that

was handy to hold a little water was a shovel. The light breeze was up-canyon so I poured water into the air from a five-gallon can and then with the shovel propped in the rocky soil so as to hold water, I stepped back. The horse did not wait long before he came to the water. We repeated this routine several times. Streak seemed not to be so wild; at least he didn't fear me. The only rope that was left in the van was three feet long. That would not help much. The horse did not move away as I walked slowly up to him. There seemed to be a little bond between us and we stood there for a while with my hand on his neck. Then Bob came huffing and puffing over the bank waving his coil of rope. The horse wheeled about and ran up the road. "Come on, Bob," I shouted as we jumped into the van. The horse ran to the end of the canyon near the aluminum cabin and stopped.

Getting out of the van, ideas of how to capture Streak were racing through my brain. The great Clark Gable and Marilyn Monroe movie, *The Misfits*, came to mind. I could just wrangle this wild one down like Gable did, mind you I knew a lot about movies, but didn't know a damn thing about horses. My friend Streak let me walk up to him again. Bob was silently watching from a safe distance. "Well, here goes!" I grabbed the horse's mane and like a real cowboy or Indian or something, I swung on his back. "Oh, my God!" What a mistake—I had not imagined what a violent and airborne ride I was in for. As Streak started making like he had just come out the chute at a rodeo all I could think was, "There are boulders in every direction and I'm going to break my neck." As much as I wanted to let go my hands would not obey. Just as suddenly I was flying through the air, fists still clenched, but there was no horse under me. By some great providence I landed, "ker thump", in an open spot between the rocks.

Shaken and stunned enough that I was still programmed to catch the horse—I had a new blur of ideas. The horse did not run away. Apparently, amazed by my attempt to fly, he stood by a safe distance from Bob and the long rope. When my eyes stopped blinking, there was the aluminum shed. It had a door on the end toward us and just one open window in the far end. Inside there was a bench full across under the window. Looking in the shed, there was a plastic tub, and now a new plan emerged. It was one that I was sure they would not use in the movies. "Let's see if we can get him in the shed." We propped the door open and with the tub filled with water placed just inside the door we waited. Bob and this horse did not seem to have any affinity for each other. Sure enough Streak plodded up and began inhaling the water. Shouting and running toward him, we hazed him into the building, slamming and latching the door. Bob surprised me by handily fashioning a halter out of a section of our rope. Streak seemed to be calm. The stable-like confine may have been a comforting reminder of a more well-fed and watered time. Bob and I crawled in on to the bench through the window, and without much difficulty we put the halter on the horse.

As the Green Machine slowly pulled away from the aluminum cabin, with Streak in tow, the idea that I would ever admit to anyone how we had captured this, sort of, wild horse was out of

Ballarat Bob with "Streak", the day we captured him at the aluminum cabin. Photo by author.

the question. Also, the idea that Bob owned this horse, or for that fact, had ever *owned* a horse was also quite remote. Of course this would not be the last time that I would be taken in by one of his stories. Later after several adventures with him, some good and others bad, I remember entering in my diary one night my opinion, "Bob is notorious for mishandling the truth." Anyway that night it was quite dark as we towed past the Anderson camp with Bob sitting in the back of the van with the doors open holding the lead rope. I stopped at my camp and I was impressed as Bob walked off into the dark, with miles to go with "his horse." But I guessed that darkness was a part of his covert act.

Author at the aluminum cabin as it looks today. Photo by Ron McKinley.

I will always imagine that Streak and I were pals. I paid Bob to get hay to fatten the animal up with and though I thought Bob wanted the horse to ride, maybe because of my flying demonstration, he never tried to ride him as far as I know. One day a young woman showed up and told me she wanted to go to Bob's (Barker claim) and ride Streak. She seemed to know what she was doing; in an open place with a lot of soft sand I put her on him bareback. The surprise was that he did not buck or kick up his heels—he just stood there and she could not get him to go anywhere, but as I walked away he followed me. So I went for a long hike around the canyon and she enjoyed riding the "wild" critter.

After a few weeks Bob came by to tell me that the Sheriff and some folks from Muscoy, California showed up at the Barker claim and took "Streak" home. There was a good possibility that Bill was compensated for boarding their lost horse but Bill did not admit that. He just said, "Boy! You're lucky, I talked 'em out of sending a posse after you for horse stealing."

THE LONGEST NIGHT

I was down in the big city (San Bernardino Valley) working at the small Rialto airport for Mr. Burt Chaffee as his maintenance supervisor when I received a call from a geologist from the Union Carbide Exploration Corporation, Richard Chamberlain. He wanted to go with me to look at the strata of tungsten ore we had discovered in the raise in the Lost Mormon Mine tunnel.

Burt's son, John, was visiting from St. Louis and I had some jobs to get out at the shop so I told Richard, "I won't be able to go to the mine until the week end but I will fly up and meet you at the air strip at the Barker Indian Ranch."

He said, "That will be fine, we can go up in my Jeep."

"I will be able to come back, when we get done. I have a van that we left at the mine camp."

"When will you get there?"

"I'll be there about noontime, O.K.?"

"O.K. See you on Saturday, Emmett."

I asked Burt if I could use the Cessna 170. "Well, we have to have it back here Saturday afternoon," he said.

"All right, how about us taking your son John with us. He can see the great Mojave Desert while he is out here. You can bring the Cessna back and I'll come home in my van as it needs some work anyhow." Burt agreed.

Yes, the van would need a fan belt but other than that it should make the trip all right. I took an overnight bag with me. In it were my jacket and vanity kit along with a couple of cans of motor oil and three different length fan belts that the help at my brother's wrecking yard had picked out for me. So, on Saturday morning, the three of us jumped into the plane and started out.

I was proud as we soared above the majestic desert scenery. I tried to point out different things to John, though he did not seem to have my enthusiasm for the Mojave. Anyway I enjoyed the flight and was excited as I descended low over the sand and boulders. The alluvial rubble spoke of ancient times when great floods washed down, scouring the flesh off the mountains. Looking down, the stately gray-green creosote bushes glided by as we turned final, lining up with the dirt strip at the ranch. I thought, "What a beautiful sight."

Burt and John taxied away and the purr of the engine and the oil can sound of the thin metal fuselage soon were gone as they took off leaving me holding my blue bag. There on that sandy opening in the brush I felt at home. Within minutes a Jeep appeared on the road from the ranch house and Richard picked me up. I had only talked to him on the phone before and this was the first time for us to meet face to face.

The irony of my landing was the story Burt related to me later. As they left, he said he and John got into a verbal fight. It seems that his son was horrified by the whole desert scene and Burt said that John shouted at him over the engine noise, "You claim to be a friend of that man so how could you leave him in the very middle of hell like that?"

Richard and I had a peaceful smooth trip down Panamint Valley and up Goler Wash. Richard was an interesting and talented geologist besides being good company on the trail. We spent the night at Russell's and then climbed up to the mine. I liked his climbing style; he believed we shouldn't take rest stops, but pace ourselves at what I would call a conversational steady stride, that is going only fast enough so we always had enough breath left to carry on a conversation. We were at the 7,000-foot level before we knew it. I enjoyed our two days even if he did not think the ore body was big enough for Union Carbide to be interested in.

It was late in the afternoon and hot as blue blazes when we came back down into camp. The shadows were already stretching out into Striped Butte Valley as I said goodbye and watched Richard's Jeep disappear around the bend on Russell's rocky road.

I stood there listening to the rise and fall of the sound of his engine as he made gear changes winding his way toward Mengel's Pass. All of a sudden it hit me, "I should have got the van going before he left!" The van was parked on a hill so even if the battery was low I thought I could get it going. "Hey! You better get moving as it will be dark soon, get the new fan belt on." I got some tools out of the box in the van and soon had the generator loose. The first belt was too short. And so were the next two. Brother Tom's helper, Speedy wasn't my best friend about that time you can guess. "Don't panic, maybe you can take the generator off of its brackets and wedge it against the engine and the longest belt will work, oops, still just a little short." I brought out the bumper jack and tried to stretch the belt. Now I was sweating and not just from the triple-digit heat.

Author making emergency field repairs to the Green Machine. Photo by Carl Ruona.

The van whirled into life; there was enough battery. With an old piece of cotton sash cord cut to the right length and stapled with bailing wire the generator was spinning merrily. "Get out of here while there is still some sunshine left." By the time I was in Warm Springs Canyon the shadows had blended into a moonless night and there were lights at the talc mine; the night shift was under way. It was even hotter at this elevation. "You should stop and see if they have a belt—I'll make it. Go on." Now that I was using the headlights it didn't look like the improvised belt was doing much good as it was slipping, and the lights were dim. I pulled out at a wide spot and let a talc truck from the mine thunder past. When I got to the Death Valley west side dirt road and turned toward the town of Baker, seventy miles away, the engine was missing, and with the lights there wasn't enough voltage for the ignition. "Oh, no." On an almost flat stretch of the road the engine died. It seemed so strange; it was a black, black night and yet there in the floor of Death Valley it was still as hot as a furnace. Thank God I had two five-gallon cans of water. "Maybe it will run without lights." It would not start.

"Oh boy, now what do you do dummy?"

In front of the van there was a very slight downgrade, not steep enough to get going fast enough to start the engine. Behind the van about a hundred feet there was a dip in this dirt haul road, a downhill stretch. After pouring water over my head and soaking my shirt, by the light of a flashlight I got out the old bumper jack. I was quite embarrassed but determined to get going. "Good God," here was the great Death Valley prospector in a really dumb predicament. I jacked up the front of the van as high as the jack would go. Pushing the jack over backwards, and at the same time sliding a rock with my foot to block the front wheel from rolling toward me, it was possible to move the machine toward the dip a few inches at a time. Doing this over and over for several sweat-soaked hours the van was on the crest of the downhill grade, but I was exhausted. It was still too dark to travel without headlights. I had conserved the flashlight using it sparingly. Really wasted and almost zombie like, one more time the jack was as high as it would go. There was no need for the rock this time! As the van rolled backwards it made a crunching sound on the gravel, the sound was so satisfying. "My God, run, jump in, throw it in gear, start it!" With the flashlight waving in one hand, running after it, I was able to wrench the door open. The engine roared into life, shattering the stillness. Parked back on the edge of the grade with the hand brake set, the feeble lash-up was spinning the generator. Maybe the battery would recover some.

West end of Anvil Canyon Wash. In the background is the west side road where the Green Machine ran out of juice. Photo by author.

Sitting there in the dark, still breathing in short spasms, I wondered where do I go from here. "You may not have enough gas to run the engine till morning and still get to Baker." At first it was a spot of light like a firefly. In a while the light got bigger and turned into two lights. "Yes! It must be a talc truck, empty on the way to the mine. Hurry, get turned around." Pulling over off the edge as far as the rock berm would allow, hoping that big lumbering truck, that sounded like a freight train coming, wouldn't turn the van, my lovely Green Machine, into so much scattered green wreckage along the haul road, I waited. Pointed downhill it was a reasonable risk to put the brakes on to light the tail lights. The truck rumbled past and did not slow down. The van pulled in close behind like it had a mind of its own. The trucks tail lights were beacons in the contrail of dust. It was time to swallow my pride. There was a yard light at the shop building. "What makes you think they would have a fan belt that will fit this old GMC?"

"Hi there, what the hell can I do for you? My name is George." He held out his hand.

I told him my dilemma; he said, "Come on in the shop, let's see what we can do." We walked into the nice metal building and he led the way to a workbench. Reaching up to an orderly row of belts hanging on the wall, he said, "There we go." I must have looked a bit bedraggled. He opened the hood of the van and in just a few minutes he slammed the hood and wiped his hands. "There you go buddy, glad I could help you." "What do I owe you?" I said. "Not a darn thing, have a good trip." The headlights were bright, but the great prospector didn't feel very bright right then.

It was daylight before I got to Baker. The two-lane asphalt roadway turned into blurry double vision and I had to pull off, falling sound asleep immediately. Sometime later, when the throbbing engine and the air blast of a passing tractor-trailer rig rocked me awake, I headed on toward Rialto and the airport.

That was a long time ago and now that talc mining camp is a deserted ghost town, a victim of overzealous politics. The canyon walls there are streaked with thick white strata. This remote spot in Death Valley, I have been told, has the largest and the finest talc deposit in North America. Nowadays when I have work to do in that area, sometimes I camp there where the stream of warm water runs between the deserted buildings and now and then I remember that hot night and the happy mechanic, George.

AIRMAIL

I heard the rattle of an old pickup coming down the gravel driveway at my house in Devore (a small mountain town in Cajon Pass, above San Bernardino, California) and I stepped out to meet my company. He was a prospector that had just come down from Butte Valley; he held a wrinkled piece of a brown paper sack out the window of his truck to me. "Carl Ruona asked me to get this to ya." I thanked him and watched his dusty truck drive out my circular drive.

Carl Ruona had scribbled the note asking me to help him. He and his wife Lucille were stuck at Russell's camp. The rear differential in his International Scout had broken. His note listed the parts he would need to repair it. This happened during a period when, because of my expertise with dynamite, I was work-

Carl Ruona astride a young mule used for packing out ore. Photo by author.

ing on a local construction project and it was difficult to take time out to drive up there and back. I had an idea that I might be able to get parts up to Russell's camp without taking that much time.

About a year before, Harry Briggs had talked me into helping him grade a landing strip at his Southern Homestead Mine; this in itself was an adventure that I will discuss later. The first airplane to land there was flown by Jim Campbell. This man was not only a fantastic bush pilot, he was also the best marksman I have ever seen (he and my wife once got into a shoot-out at Briggs's camp, a target shoot-out). This guy had the skill and dexterity to be able to toss a coin in the air, draw an Old West six-shooter and hit the coin while it was still spinning high in the air. Speaking of high, Jim was impressive, well over six feet tall. His large handlebar mustache added to his dignified image.

If anyone could help me airdrop a package to Carl, it would have to be someone like him. That night, Thursday, I called him at home in Los Angeles to see if he would be interested in the airdrop rescue.

"I can't do it tonight, Emmett."

"No, no, Jim, I was thinking about this Saturday."

"Where can I pick you up?"

"How about at the Rialto Airport."

"Emmett, I'll be there at 6:30 A.M., O.K.?"

This was the same man that had flown Harry Briggs to Ash Meadows, Nevada for his eighty-second birthday.

Ruth took me to the airport and we got there early, but Jim was already there, standing by his shiny Cessna 170. I looked around nervously as we loaded the two bundles. We snugly strapped them into the rear seat. I looked around again, sure that if drug agents were monitoring air traffic here at Rialto our activities would appear suspicious.

As an engineer I had thought about this kind of an aerial delivery before; now was my chance to try it. I only had one day to find the parts and set things up and as it turned out the first part was a cinch. The dealership had everything we needed. I fit the parts into two fifty-caliber ammunition cans. The plastic bottles of lubricant I froze and bundled up with cakes of dry ice. Everything was packed solid; each square metal can was then wrapped in a blue un-inflated and inexpensive air mattress. Then I lashed each bundle with white nylon parachute cord.

It was still morning when the ghost town of Ballarat appeared in the desert haze. The colors, light brown, gray and green were vivid. Jim came in low over remnants of the once bustling town. There were only a few cars, some derelict, near the store building. There was a dim track of a diagonal lane cutting thru some of the old adobe walls. The Cessna glided in almost noiseless until the wheels touched down, then there was the familiar metallic rumble of the aluminum fuselage and the whirring of the prop as Jim taxied aside.

"Hi, Paul, how's things going?"

"Emmett, it's you, I never know how you're going to show up."

"Paul, Like you to meet Jim Campbell."

"You guys want me to look after the plane for you?"

"NO! No we just stopped to see if we could get some coffee and maybe some scrambled eggs, Paul, then we are going on to Butte Valley. Thanks."

Our next stop was actually a dry lakebed high up in Middle Park, in the top of the mountain range. At the lakebed we were a bit higher and north of Russell's camp, so it was safe to inflate the air mattresses around the ammunition cans. I got dizzy, orally blowing them up at this altitude. I only staggered a little as we took the right-hand door off the plane; Jim laughed. We pushed the front passenger seat all the way forward with the back tilted ahead. The discarded door we set aside in a safe place and weighted it down with large rocks. I strapped myself in the back seat with the packages on the floor and the seat to my left. When we flew out over Butte Valley, the monument, the Butte that was once sediment millions of years ago in an ocean floor, now protruded hundreds of feet into the sky in the center of Shangri-La. In the morning light its colored bands were startling.

We headed south flying straight over the three camps that were lined up and huddled into the foot of the east slope of Manly

Peak. The Stone Cabin, then Greater View where Carl Mengel used to live, and next, southernmost, nestled into a narrow wash, was Russell's camp. Jim buzzed the camp a few hundred feet above it, but he had to pull up steeply as we were flying right into the east wall of Manly. I had a brief glimpse of Carl Ruona's International Scout, propped up in the parking area, as we shot by. "Jim, I don't think we can get very close. It is too tight."

"No, that isn't tight, watch this." About now I may have been holding my breath. He headed back toward the Butte and then did a wingover and headed back diving and paralleling the camps, flying close to the mountain on our right—real close. There is a small ridge between Greater View and Russ's. We just cleared it and Jim dropped down and headed out following the wheel ruts of the driveway. We were now headed away from Manly but the wings were almost brushing the boulders on either side. Everything was a blur; the wind was tugging at my goggles. The walls of the wash magnified the mean sound of the prop. We were so low I looked at Carl, who was standing at the side of the road, eye-to-eye. As I tossed the payload out the open door, I prayed that the packages would clear the tail of the plane. I threw them toward the ground so hard it was a good thing my seat belt was tight or I could have gone out too.

As a matter of fact Carl later told me, "Emmett, what da hell, I taught you were going to just step out."

The air was smooth as we landed at Middle Park and recovered the door.

There was more excitement ahead. Our return trip was not boring.

That morning after we left the airport in Rialto it had been necessary for us to radio air traffic control as our flight path from Cajon Pass on a straight line to Ballarat would take us through a restricted air space. Traffic Control would ordinarily give permission, but that day they wouldn't. We had to go around the Palmdale area to the west, much farther. Going home we were in a hurry and Jim said, "I don't want to fly that detour around Palmdale. Let's fly just high enough to stay out of the power lines and we will be able to stay under their radar."

"O.K., we can stay to one side of Highway 395 and that will save us a lot of time."

We weren't much higher than the brush most of the way back. I hope we weren't being tracked by radar by the boys at air traffic control.

When Jim made his final approach to Miro Field, Rialto airport, he had a strong crosswind to contend with, and touching down it was necessary to use a lot of cross brake to keep the plane on the runway; it was a tense moment. Just when we were below flying speed, all hell broke loose, the right brake failed. The plane ground-looped, the scenery spun wildly, we just missed hitting a plane on the taxiway.

Jim regained control and slowly we pulled to a parking area. "Jim, now what?"

"I think we sheared the stationary disks on the right brake. You won't believe this but the only thing in the baggage compartment is a barbeque grate and a set of new disks."

"Jim, I have connections here as I used to manage a maintenance facility here. I know the Miro family. We probably will be able to borrow a jack and tools and get you on your way in a hurry. It will be legal as I have an FFA airplane mechanic license."

I was nervous, hoping we had slipped through the radar net O.K., and now there was the possibility that someone would want a written report about our little ground-loop escapade on the runway. I walked into the maintenance shop with Jim and shook hands with some old friends and soon we had the jack and the hand-tools to fix the plane. Even though the wind was cool, I was sweating.

Jim was just taxiing away and my wife was standing with me, ready to take me home, when a small delegation of men in business suits came up to me. Sam Miro, Jr. introduced us and we shook hands all around. I wondered what was going on. Sam, said, "Hi, good to see you again, Emmett. The airport has sure changed, huh? Emmett, I would like to show you and Ruth our new boardroom."

Ruth and I were escorted into the building and into a very

elegant large room with a large conference table in the middle. One of the men there was introduced to me as a friend of Sam's who was visiting from out of town. The way he was dressed, the suit, the haircut, and then, when he placed a chart on the table and started asking me about where I was able to land in the desert, I knew! I had seen enough movies, and this was your typical FBI agent. "Thanks, Sam, glad to meet you all, but really, my wife has an appointment, I'm sorry but we have to go." I was surprised, no one snapped out a pair of handcuffs, they were just pleasant and gave us a cordial goodbye.

The big surprise came Tuesday in the newspaper. A new airplane had crashed in the desert near Barstow Sunday night and it had been based at the Miro Field. As I read further, the plane had apparently run out of fuel looking for a place to land. The crash site was near Barstow, way out in the desert. In the wreckage they found a half-ton of marijuana. Not far from the crash they found the body of a man that may have been the pilot. He was an airlines pilot from Canada, sadly enough he was the same man I had met at the airport that I thought had been an FBI agent.

So much for the movies.

BEFORE YOU GO INTO THE DESERT READ THIS

KEEP THE DOOR LATCHED

When I headed out on my first trip to Panamint City in the 1950s I was still a young man. I had read several exciting things about this famous old ghost town that was located high up in the Panamint Range, just below the highest peak on the west side of Death Valley. This high point is called Telescope Peak and it is over 11,000 feet above sea level.

Panamint City had been a flourishing mining camp in the 1870s and for a few years it had produced tons of silver. However when I decided to go there it had been abandoned for over eighty years!

I was particularly interested in seeing if I could find the section of the graveyard that had been named Bruce's Graveyard. There was a fanciful story about Bruce, a mild-mannered faro dealer that the local bullies had decided to pick on. It seems he had shot several of the local toughs in a series of gunfights and that there was a separate section just for his victims.

Anyway I headed out one afternoon by myself, leaving my wife and our small children home. For this adventure I was driving a 1931 Model A Ford coupe. I had bought the Ford from a customer at my brother Tom's auto wrecking yard for fifty dollars. It was in less than perfect condition. Instead of a trunk lid it had a wooden box sticking out of the trunk, sort of a mini pickup bed. The engine ran good but the gear train made sort of a growling sound and it seemed to be the happiest if I kept the speed down to under fifty miles an hour.

It was slow going, so it was very late when the lights of the town of Trona, on the edge of Searles Lake (dry), were still on the horizon. It was time to pull over and get some sleep. It had been a long day. Pulling off in a wide sandy spot I was soon stretched out in my sleeping bag and sound asleep.

The sun's bold light spread across the morning sky outlining the dark angles of the horizon while it was still hidden. It was going to be a hot day. I was up and moving in the shadows. The old Ford faithfully purred into life and the sleeping city of Trona was soon behind me. Between Searles Valley and Panamint Valley the road swings up over the top and then it steeply twists its way down the eastside of the Slate Range. The Ford boldly climbed to the top and when it started down I decided that it could coast down to flatland at the bottom of the grade. It would probably roll along faster maybe. It was a lot quieter out of gear— no grinding sound. Smooth, peaceful, it was almost as if the Ford was floating down into the valley. All I had to do was spin the steering wheel back and forth, negotiating the turns. In a stretch where there was a bit of straightaway, I sat back in the seat and unlatched the door and propped it open with my foot. The morning air was still sort of cool and with the door ajar there was a nice breeze batheing the inside of the car. There wasn't any other creature or vehicle in sight.

WHAM! The Ford ran into an invisible wall. I was thrown violently against the steering wheel. Dumbfounded, pushing myself back in the seat I saw in the rearview mirror a trail of smoke behind and I realized what had happened—the rear wheels had locked up. It was paramount in my mind that I should skid the car to the side so as not to block the road.

That was definitely a bad move! Skidding toward the edge— the car suddenly spun out from under me. The open door slapped against my backside and then I was airborne above the pavement for a short distance, landing relatively softly on my hands and knees in the middle of the roadway.

Stunned, one moment I had been part of the modern world, traveling in my own noisy mechanical capsule, part of man's mastery of the world, then without any prelude I found I was really alone. Robbed of all my superiority, as if I had slipped into another dimension; I had been captured by this peaceful quiet, beautiful desert morning. There were only those ghost-like vaporous sounds, the rocks and the bugs coming to life in the heat of the early morning sun. The view out over Panamint Valley, still below me, was awesome. I was of course quite embarrassed, having been deposited there so ignobly. Completing my amazement was the fact that the Ford had disappeared completely. I got to my feet, and for a while I just stood there. It was hard to believe that I was not hurt except where the door had slammed into my butt. Little did I know that there was going to be a series of more surprises ahead for me while pursuing this once boisterous ghost town.

When I walked over to the edge of the road and looked down the steep slope toward the floor of the valley, about two hundred feet below me the Ford, having gathered a crowd of rocks and small boulders around it as it careened down, had stopped, its self-destruct bent had been arrested.

With the rocks pulled out from underneath and cleared away it looked like it would be possible to drive down the rest of the hillside where it gave way to a sandy wash, and if that worked then there was a natural path down the wash into the valley and back onto the road. But how about the jammed-up running gear?

Being tenacious and not willing to yet accept the idea that I had been rudely cast afoot into this bleak desert, I vigorously set about to try to recover my vehicle. Clearing the rocks away was easy. When I got in and pushed the starter pedal there was a loud clanking noise under the hood. When we had slammed into that invisible wall, the car horn had slid forward on the radiator stabilizer rod to where, when the engine turned over, the fan blade would hit it. It did not take long to fix that and soon the engine was running. But when I let out the clutch the engine stalled, the rear end was still locked up.

Shifting the transmission into reverse did it! CLUNK! The wheels would roll now. Back in first gear I drove down, taking care not to turn far to either side, making gentle turns around boulders, so as not to get sideways and turn the car over on the steep slope.

It worked and back on the pavement I soon came to the dirt road that headed off to the east across a dry lake.

The dried mud of the lakebed, with the shadow of the high mountain range to the east retreating like a horizontal curtain, was already reflecting the morning sun. On the far side of the lake a few adobe walls and an out-building or two was all that was left of Ballarat, a town that had sported several saloons back in the 1890s, during its heyday. I was still only interested in getting to Panamint City. There was no time to look around. Turning left on what had once been the main drag the old mine camp was left behind. The Ford was chugging upgrade on the dirt road that would lead to the mouth of Surprise Canyon and the fabulous steep mining road that would climb over six thousand feet in about eight miles—to Panamint City.

Just as I was passing a large grove of mesquite trees that had once been a thriving Indian camp before the white man came, the Ford started doing strange things. The engine was speeding up but the car was slowing down. What the hell! This wasn't a very steep grade yet, but the Ford didn't want to go up it. As it turned out the engine was spinning the axle but not one rear wheel. I guessed that when the differential had locked up coming down into the valley the key that locks the wheel to the axle had been sheared.

Well, there were just a few old tools in the car, three wrenches, a pair of pliers and a file. And, oh yes, there was a jack and a wheel wrench, too. "Hardly enough to do any repairs here in the middle of this dusty mine road," I said to myself. After scratching my head a bit I found out that one of the wrenches, a big box open-end wrench, fit the axle nut. I thought that if the nut were tightened forcing the wheel onto the tapered end of the axle tight enough, maybe the wheel wouldn't slip even though the key had been broken. Putting the tool on so the handle stuck out horizontally and standing on it tightened the nut with a great amount of tension.

Once again the engine was purring and the Ford was continuing up the road. Yes, it was a bit scary and there was a lot of steep road ahead. Little did I know that I was tightening myself into more of a dilemma, obsession is often not a good thing.

Even before the Surprise Canyon road it was necessary to stop and tighten the axle nut some more. The axle was smoking, almost red hot and it was being stretched. But on I went, the Ford easily going up the canyon toward the city, that is, when the rear wheel wasn't spinning loose. But by tightening it several times I got to the edge of the old Panamint ghost town and then it happened!

The heated metal had stretched as far as it would go, the nut couldn't be tightened any more; the axle was free to spin; the car would not go a foot farther. Undaunted, I remembered seeing some pieces of rusty scrap metal along the edge of the road a ways back and I did have a file so maybe I could fashion a new axle key. But would the wheel come off? Yes, the Ford was blocking the road but it was not likely anyone else would be along this way for weeks.

There were many good-sized rocks on either side of the road berm. When the car was jacked up and firmly blocked up with some of these, I was able to use one large rock for a sledge hammer, and surprise, surprise, off came the wheel. The slipping of the wheel on the axle had so polished the metal that it was almost impossible to see where the keyway had been. After using a rock to hammer on the file, using it as a chisel, the halves of the fractured axle key came free, out of the keyway. Looking at the two pieces of metal in my hand, and contemplating how to create a new key, a thought came to me. It was like someone was whispering in my ear, maybe one of the blacksmiths from the ghost camp, "Just turn the pieces of the old key together sideways and put them back in the slot." I soon had everything together again; would it work? I was somewhat chagrined when I realized that I had been operating like the ancient aborigine, using rocks for my tools.

The illustrious Ford coupe did just fine and I went right into the middle of the old town; turning left, I went up the side canyon where the old newspaper stories said the graveyard would be. There I set up my little camp. My small one-burner propane-can stove had a pot of tea boiling in a matter of minutes. It had taken me quite a while with all the trouble I had encountered to arrive at the graveyard location, but there was still enough of the day left to thoroughly search the area. There was the main graveyard and off to the side there was a separate section that I presumed was assigned to the loser of gunfights with Bruce, the faro dealer. I was thrilled to have touched some of the history of the old west and none too soon, the headboards on the graves were already so weathered that you could only faintly make out some of the names. It would not be long before the markers themselves would disappear.

That night I thought there wasn't another living soul around anywhere for many, many miles. I slept soundly. Later I learned that had I continued on up beyond the ghost town a short distance I would have come to the camp of "Shotgun Mary," a hanger-on from the old days, who was famous for taking shots at prospectors that happened to get too close to what she considered her territory, legal or otherwise. On a subsequent trip I did meet her and was able to talk her out of shooting me!

The next day I really enjoyed prowling around and I got through the day without any company until that afternoon. As it turned out, my younger brother Robert found out that I had gone into a mysterious part of the desert alone and he decided that I would need to be rescued. At least that was the excuse he gave for heading out to see if he could find me. You can imagine my surprise when I heard, and then saw, a 1950 Oldsmobile sedan coming my way.

Robert and his friend Clancy Fulton arrived in a cloud of dust; they had been burning up the road with their high-power vehicle. They soon ridiculed my car and my camp. They got a big kick out of seeing the row of used tea bags that were hanging on the stabilizer bar that ran across between the headlights on the Ford. "I was running short, going to recycle some you see," I explained.

Well I ended up with the last laugh that day. When we got ready to leave, I found out that my rescuers were almost out of gas. I had an extra five-gallon army can full in the open trunk of the Ford and that was enough to get them back to town.

My adventure did not stop when I left Panamint City. Robert and Clancy vanished in a cloud of smoke from their spinning tires when we got to the pavement. I made my way back through the great desert at a very modest pace, the Ford purring along at a fast 55 MPH. Not far south of the almost deserted old mining town of Red Mountain, out along a barren stretch of Highway 395, I saw a very well dressed older man standing by the side of the road. He wore a nice suit and had two expensive-looking leather suitcases. This guy was miles from anything and there had been no sign of a car on or off the road since the last town.

I thought, "No way can I leave anyone afoot out here," so I stopped. He eagerly tossed his luggage into the makeshift truck bed in the back and climbed in and latched the door without saying a word. I glanced at him and he did look a bit familiar. I put the old car into gear and we were grinding merrily along. After about twenty miles he asked, "Are you taking this car to town to an auto wrecking yard?" Somehow his question irked me. Even if I had reprieved it from my brother's yard and that was probably where it was going to end up, and even if I did have a big beautiful Cadillac Fleetwood sitting in my driveway at home I felt like he was being a bit audacious. Why bad-mouth the old Ford, after all, it had just rescued him. So I lied, "No, this is my only car!" We didn't talk any more. When I pulled in at the Out Post gas station just before Cajon Pass he got out to stretch while I put gas in the car. When I was ready to leave, before he could get back in, I set his luggage out on the pavement beside him. "Aren't you going on over the pass?" he asked. "Yes, I am. But that old tired Ford isn't strong enough to haul the two of us any farther," I replied.

When I got down the road a ways, I felt like a fool. That had been a rude, stupid gesture on my part. To this day I don't feel good about it. He probably didn't mean to insult my car.

Years later when the story came out about a guy picking up a hitchhiker that turned out to be the multimillionaire Howard Hughes, I tried hard to remember what the man I had left standing at the Out Post station looked like.

BE PREPARED

One day Mr. Briggs and I were going up his South Park Canyon Road in my Dodge army surplus 4WD ½-ton truck (this is the same mining road where Mr. Briggs had lost a truck over the side once, the wreckage is still at the bottom of the draw).

Before we were up to his Banta Camp mill site he said, "I want to show you the Suitcase Mine. See that turnout ahead? Turn left and it will take us up there. I want to see if you think there is any more gold ore to be developed there."

I wanted to see the Suitcase Mine all right. I knew that the Banta Mill had been built to process the gold from there and that the mine had been a family operation that had made better than wages for the Banta family all during the Great Depression of the 1930s. I had interviewed George Higer and as a young man he had helped build the camp and had poured gold into ingots there. He said, "Some of the ore was so rich with free-milling gold that you could just shake the rock and little grains of gold would fall out in your hand."

The road to the mine did not look safe to me. The farther I drove the narrower it became. The drop-off on my side was straight down for hundreds of feet, and like some of the South Park Road it had been blasted across the vertical side of a canyon. Only this road obviously was built to accommodate a wagon, Model T Ford, or maybe just pack animals. At least it was so tight a squeeze for my army truck that I said, " Harry, I don't think we can make it with this truck, this must have been made for a Model T." He said, "Oh, you will make it O.K., just keep going!"

I still didn't like it, as I could see our wheels were running too close to the edge; I imagined I could hear the road crumbling off into the abyss behind us.

Then I stole a glance at Mr. Briggs. Even though he kept encouraging me to keep going, the door on his side was unlatched and he was perched ready to abandon our vehicle at a moment's notice.

On the return trip, now that my side was the uphill side, I drove as close to the inside as I could, almost scraping the side of the truck against the natural rock wall. Yes, my door was un-latched this time.

On our way to the Banta Camp he said, "I suppose that if we want to do any more work back there at the mine, we might want to bulldoze another road, cross-country from the mill, huh?"

DON'T TURN YOUR BACK

I have made this mistake that I'm going to put down here three times. This is not a record and it sure isn't something to brag about either. I want to write about it because even though this thing is stupid, others in the wilderness have gotten into deep trouble the same way.

Another prospector I have known for years and have respect for his tenacity and daring, wanted me to go with him to help him dynamite and dig in one of his secret mining claims. We will call him Sam. Though Sam worked in an office in Los Angeles, California, and wasn't real robust, he was so intrigued by the mysteries and forgotten diggings left by the earlier treasure hunters that he escaped into the badlands whenever he had a chance. Sam is the only other person I know that has prowled the south end of Death Valley like I have. Like myself, he has often allowed his zeal, curiosity, and determination to overcome good sense. The following story is an example of what can happen if you put two mad prospectors together in the same area.

Sam's secret diggings were not easy to get to. They were high above Redlands Canyon. It was necessary to come in from the north. First, up South Park mining road to the top of the range and then drive down a wash that had never had a road in it, dodging boulders and gullies, going through heavy creosote brush for over a mile, then leave the Jeep and climb up the wall of a canyon to a cliff face. Around the buttress and then taking a ridge to where it angled into another sharp ridgeline, then you came to the prospect overlooking the whole Panamint Valley.

We went in Sam's Jeep. It was cold and late when we got to the top of the range. We decided to stay in a cabin that was sheltered in the pine trees up there, Madeleine MacDougel's camp I believe it was called. There was plenty of firewood stockpiled there and cots to sleep on and it didn't look like anyone had been there in a while.

There was another mine cabin a little over a quarter of a

mile away that we could see. It was a little lower, across a brush-covered plain, but there was no sign of life there. That is until our visitor arrived. We called him Pal for the want of a better name—a big black Labrador. It was obvious he belonged to the other camp and had been left there.

Pal was happy to see someone and he moved right in with us and when we got the fifty-gallon barrel stove going he lay down in front of it and stayed there all night as our sentry.

In the morning there was a problem. Pal was going with us whether or no. We would have a time just packing water for ourselves and we would be climbing in the rocks. Besides that, even though it had been a cold night at this high altitude it was still summer in Death Valley and during the day the sun would blaze down without mercy. As the saying goes, "Only mad dogs and Englishmen go out in the noonday sun." I thought Sam and I could handle it even if we were not Englishmen, but it would be a miserable day for Pal on our hike.

We could not have him with us so we tricked him. We started out driving down the road toward his camp. It worked. He was smart and as soon as he saw which way we were going he raced off on a shortcut toward the camp. When Pal was out of sight in the tall sage, Sam made a U-turn and we were soon off the road and headed down the craggy wash hidden from the top of the range.

It was slow going and Sam carefully threaded the Jeep between the hazards. We were about a half-mile into this secret route when Pal caught up to us. He was one disappointed and tired Lab, his tongue hanging out. I gave him water and we had to put him on the tailgate of the Jeep. He was going with us after all.

If I had guessed how it was going to turn out I'd have put the dog in my seat and turned back myself!

Sam, after struggling through the main wash, turned south into a smaller tributary canyon and in a short distance he stopped. Leaving the Jeep we slung on our backpacks and I took along a round-pointed shovel as well. And with Pal, sometimes ahead, sometimes behind, we started up the steep hillside. It was very steep and when we got near the crest of the slope we came to a natural buttress that provided us with a place out of the sun and a flat area where we could get our breath back before gaining the ridge. Already the sun was beginning to bear down on our little patrol. The ridge we followed was quite narrow and cluttered by large granite boulders and a scant growth of greasewood brush. It seemed to head due west and Pal led the way. Sam showed us an ancient gold prospect and then we turned south around the crest of another hilltop. It was early enough that shadows clung to the slope and we could now see the beautiful panorama of Panamint Valley spread out on our right side, way below. Ribbons and vales of salt-incrusted silt were waiting for the next cloudburst to revive the salt waste into a muddy sea and settle the dusty vapors.

We arrived at Sam's secret prospect. We worked quite a while to accomplish his annual assessment work, blasting and mucking into a promising quartz vein.

By the time we headed back "Old Sol" was well in its glory and things were heating up considerably. The shadows had gone into hiding on the slope and Pal was now a little more frugal in his meandering, as the ground was getting warmer. On the floor of Panamint Valley below there were now shimmering mirages, magic waterless pools.

Sam pointed out to me a weathered post along our route and said, "I think this may be where an old prospector used to tie his burro." After looking closely around this artifact I told him, "This looks to me like some of the sites I've found where they had a bellows for tool sharpening—there may be a mine close by." We climbed down the slope a short distance and sure enough there was another old diggings.

Back on the narrow ridge the air was still and there was only the sound of the three of us crunching along. You could smell the heat as it bounced off the rocks. Pal was having a bad time of it, the sun was straight overhead and he was trying to find shady places to walk in without much success. He wasn't the only one in trouble either. In the middle of that stretch Sam decided he couldn't go any farther.

As I said earlier, Sam was used to being under cover, working in an office. "I can't go on, I've got to stop here. There is a big boulder here with a dent in it where I can get out of the sun," he said.

Well, yes, there was a shadow, but there was just room for him, even Pal couldn't squeeze in with him. As I swung around there wasn't another spot of shade to be found anywhere. I stood there a bit dumbfounded as Sam retreated leaving Pal and I ablaze in the noonday sun. I finally said, "Sam, Pal and I will go on ahead and when we get to that buttress at the point of the hill, ya know where we stopped on the way up? We'll be in the shade there and wait for you, after you cool down a bit, O.K.?" Sam croaked, "Yes."

There was a nice shady ledge at the point and I wished Sam had made it there with us. I took off my boots and cooled my feet. I poured water from the canteen into the cup of the shovel for pal to drink and he seemed mighty grateful. He lay down beside me, my buddy, ya know. We were there quite a while and I finally became worried. Sam should have caught up by now I thought. Maybe he had heatstroke or a heart attack. I laced up my boots and stepped back out into the yellow fire. Pal, as painful as it was for him, went right along with me. We could not be sure we were back to the right boulder now that the noon hour had passed. There was no one there! O my God! "Sam, Sam, Sam," I called out. Then remembering another disaster where the injured party had rolled off the side of a mountain while writhing in pain, I went as far over the edge as I could, almost slipping in the loose rocks; maybe he caught on a ledge, "Sam, Sam. Sam." Now I was getting panicky. Delirious, did he turn back to his mine? I retraced our route. What the hell had happened to him? We had waited where he would have had to pass us.

My face flushed and salt from sweating stung my eyes. My core temperature was way up. I wasn't far from a heatstroke of my own. Then I made my next mistake. Pal and I were back near the infamous dented boulder and as I wiped my brow with my checker handkerchief I jokingly called out to Pal, who was behind me, "Why don't you go and find Sam?" In the blaze of the sun I stood there trying to come up with an idea of what to do; it was terrible. The poor man needs help but I can't find him. When

I turned around to look at Pal he was gone, not a sign of him.

I had a notion Pal had gone off to the south of the point. Maybe he had gone on to the Jeep that way. Well I felt sure that if I went down to the vehicle there was no way in my condition that I could climb back to the ridge. I would have to go for help. There was a lot of brush and the slope was still so steep that I could not see the Jeep until I was almost on top of it.

There was Pal—and Sam! He had the back hatch up and was casually fixing himself a snack. "What the hell happened to you?" "Oh, I came around the other side. Funny thing, we had the same mix-up when I was out here with my boy last year."

It wouldn't have taken too much right then for the occurrence of another mysterious death in the Panamints!

LOOK FOR THE GOOD GUYS

Using a string of pack animals is one way to get gold off the top of a remote mountaintop and I am glad that I had that invaluable experience. One of the old-time rangers that came to our camp once when we were unloading the burros one day said, "Emmett, you guys are the only ones in Death Valley operating a mine like they did a hundred years ago."

Well, that same day I found the vein in Redlands Canyon and had been sitting there remembering the "Lost Dutchman Story." I was about to switch to a more high-tech method of gold recovery. Not only did I strike raw gold that day but I was soon to meet someone that would not only help me with the gold but become a good friend. I would be amazed by his skill and cool nerve.

The throbbing beat of a helicopter startled me out of the Dutchman's spell. It was a strange sound in these parts. This was "my" part of Death Valley. For years the hard-to-get-to places around Manly Peak had been pretty much my own kingdom.

I was curious as to what was going on here in "my canyon." The helicopter did not sound far away. Maybe there was a chance to get near enough to see. My van was parked in the brush on the floor of the canyon, three hundred feet below, at the beginning of the faint new trail to the gold-impregnated quartz outcrop. I tossed the pick and shovel into the opening of the pit I had dug and jogged down through the rocks and cactus. The twisting trail brought me to where I could see my green van. It looked like a toy in the wash below. Once in the van I headed up-canyon toward the "Invaders."

On the way I passed by the road to my current base camp. My camp was a five-acre mill site, a mile away, on the north side of Manly Peak. At this designated spot there was a small aluminum cabin with a fancy outhouse, a lone pine tree and a water tank. These luxuries were situated in the middle of a narrow flood plain where violent cloudbursts eons ago had left behind rather impressive pieces of the surrounding alpine grandeur. The camp was very isolated, out of sight from the road until you are within 150 feet of it from the air. Of course, the aluminum building was like a solar beacon. To get up to my place you had to take the side road and climb steeply through a maze of boulders, twisting back and forth like a snake. There were seldom any visitors and my main company at that refuge was an owl and a noisy badger. The badger always banged rudely into the metal wall of the cabin on its way around the structure during its regular nightly trek. I don't know why it did this, maybe to show its contempt for someone building an obstacle in the path, or he, or she, might have just been clumsy. There used to be wild burros around all the time, usually coming in close to graze in the evening; these magnificent creatures were the nomads left over from an earlier period. The first prospectors had formed partnerships with their progenitors. The burro became an icon in the West. Sometimes these prowlers would wake me up, braying loudly, in the middle of the night, but the camp had gotten quieter. The government had initiated a program to remove the herds. More about the burros later.

Going up Redlands Canyon to check out the helicopter, I was wondering who was out there and what they might be doing. Were they "high grading" some "old-timer's" diggings I had not found? Then my mind drifted to the idea of how wonderful it would be to be able to have a helicopter to use. It would be a great help to go up to the lost mine I had found earlier, way up the mountain, above my aluminum cabin, at the 7,000-foot level. It took two hours to backpack up there.

The formal boundary line around Death Valley National Monument at that time was an imaginary line that bisected the mountain ranges bordering the great valley. Halfway up Redlands Canyon (named, not because of the color, but because a man from Redlands, California, worked there among the first prospectors), running north and south across the dirt road was this important line. There the natural drainage divides, to the west the rains drain down the canyon toward Panamint Valley and to the east they flow into Striped Butte Valley.

When I drove up to the boundary, I saw the helicopter had landed. It was a B3 helicopter, the same model as we used to see on the *Mash* TV series—a large plastic bubble up front with a seat inside for three people. Extending behind the bubble was a tubular framework, a skeleton that supported the bubble, the engine, rotor, tail rotor and so forth. This whole device was suspended three feet off the ground by two parallel metal skids. It looked so fragile and out of place in this natural wilderness. I was soon to find out though, that riding in this helicopter was like riding on a magic carpet—you could see everything!

They had landed 50 feet north of the road. The crew was loading some equipment on board. One of the men there came toward me. He was lithe and trim, better than average height. His posture and gait gave me the idea that here was someone I would like to know. I got out of the van and walked through the wax-coated creosote brush toward him. This was another lucky day for me. This man, who almost always had a smile on his face, was to play a most important role in my Death Valley odyssey.

He shook my hand and said, "My name is Don Landells."

"I'm Emmett Harder. I have a camp down-canyon on the north side of Manly Peak."

"I've seen your camp many times—my crew and I are working on a project for the Department of Interior, marking points along the monument boundaries that will show up on new aerial maps."

We talked for a while. Soon I decided Don and his people

were not going to be a threat. I told him I had been working a prospect down-canyon and came up to see what was happening. He was quite friendly, saying "I'm glad to meet you, Emmett, I think what you're doing is very interesting." I told him the feeling was mutual, "It must be something to fly around in that thing all day and get paid for it, too." Don gave me the idea that he admired me and my current lifestyle. Before I left him to his work I said, "Why don't

Don Landells, owner of Landells Aviation in Palm Springs, CA.. In the author's opinion one of the best helicopter pilots in the business. Picture taken in the late 1960s.

you come to my camp sometime?" "Heck, Emmett, if I can get a cup of coffee I will be there tomorrow morning, all right?"

"You have a deal, Don. It will be camp coffee, but it will be hot."

On the way back to my camp, I wondered if he could get his helicopter down near the cabin. There were large boulders, some bigger than a car, scattered about close to the cabin in the narrow wash. Sometime later, I built a heliport landing pad, but at that time the only level spot was a little clearing by a hitching rail north of the cabin, and there were blocks of granite over six feet high close by.

There is more than a bit of paranoia that goes along with the lifestyle of a prospector. This is especially true if you think you have something covetable. It was a relief to me to find out that these helicopter people were not after some of "my gold" after all—well, that's what they said anyway. I was filled with a new excitement. Maybe there was a chance to get some supplies up to the top of the mountain, so I'd be able to do some serious work up at the Lost Mormon Mine. We had been held up for a long time from proceeding because we needed quite a bit of gear up there to develop a pocket of high-grade in the raise. And just then time was of the essence; the Department of Interior had suspended my special use permit and was trying to take away my mining claim.

They were not just after Carl and me; it was a nationwide effort, not only to get rid of all the small miners, but in the same ballpark there was a real problem with people holding mining claims illegally, using them to build houses or vacation retreats on them, and they made it bad for everyone.

The Department of Interior had already taken me to court and I had to post bail. They claimed I was in violation of my special-use permit—they used the excuse that Carl had admitted that he had used a small bulldozer to improve a bad section of the road in Butte Valley. They said, "It may have improved the road but you didn't have a permit." Carl was desperate, and not thinking this was any big deal, he said, "Emmett has a permit and I did it for him." "Ah-ha! We wanted to hear you say that—his permit does not allow him to fix any roads. We've got him now." Suspending the permit put me in a unique position. With my special use-permit in limbo, I was not bound by my agreement to coordinate my activity with the Department. Under the 1872 mining laws, it was legal to mine my own valid claim. However, if they found out I was up there working the mine, there were other ways to stop me.

Somehow I needed to get set up to mine and ship the tungsten and gold ore. It had turned out to be high-grade enough to sell as sample rock. It did not need to be milled.

That evening at the aluminum cabin, I rushed around camp building a pallet that could be airlifted and loaded it with tools and supplies. The sun was well hidden behind the mountain by the time I had the rigging for a harness contrived. That night, as I lay on the army cot in the cabin, I was awake a long time planning, hoping and dreaming of getting a chance to develop that pocket of ore that was now begging me to take it to the bank.

The natural gouge on the north side of Manly Peak, where my little cabin was, was so deep that the sun came up late and went down early. That next morning at first light smoke was floating up from the tin shepherd's stove in the cabin when the staccato rhythm of the helicopter filled the canyon. Don Landells lowered his mechanical marvel down among the boulders not 100 feet from the cabin. He had come alone. He climbed out of his wonderful machine and left it running. As we walked into the cabin, he said, "I set the engine rpm so that the rotor blades will stay above the boulders. If I shut it down, the rotor blades will sink into them."

In the cabin Don sat at the little red and white checked, oil-cloth-covered table calmly drinking his coffee while the helicopter purred away down by my hitching rail. I thought, "Wow, he is taking a chance with someone's helicopter—this guy is one cool customer." Later, I learned he not only was the owner, he had more than one.

As it turned out Don was one of the very best helicopter pilots in the country and he was the owner of Landells Aviation. He had other helicopters and pilots working for him out of his heliport ranch located in Desert Hot Springs just north of Palm Springs, California. Don had been the chief pilot during the construction of the fantastic Palm Springs Tramway—an engineering marvel that transports people to the top of the highest mountain in the San Jacinto Mountains.

I relaxed as we sat talking next to the tin stove with our steaming cups of coffee. Don was quite sure of himself. He was very articulate and yet modest and talked with a soft, distinct voice. Don will always be one of my heroes. My nickname for him is "Jack Armstrong." Before TV, in the days of radio, Jack Armstrong was the All-American Hero.

I finally got the courage to ask Don, "Can that flying burro of yours lift a pallet?"

He said "Yes, there is an attachment for a sling and at this altitude I can work with a 600-pound cargo."

"Well, I have lashed up a bunch of stuff I would sure like to get up to a lost mine I found up top," I said, while waving my hand toward the jagged landscape we could see through the cabin's rear window. (That scene always reminds me of the Swiss Alps.) He put his cup down and said, "Let's take a look at what you have to get up there."

We went around behind the cabin to the lash-up of gear. It looked a bit like an overloaded, crudely built dog sled. Don studied my improvised contrivance for a while and then said, " If you're ready now, let's see if we can drag this treasure down to the copter." I ran, grabbed my hat and latched the cabin door. The load was heavy, but it slid easily downhill in the soft, decomposed granite. Don climbed in the helicopter and opened the latch for the sling as I crawled underneath to hook it up.

The air was still cool and the combined aroma of wild sage and creosote was strong. The whirling blades of the helicopter stirred the desert perfume.

As we lifted up and headed down-canyon, I had my first lesson about the delicate balance of a helicopter. Don, speaking loudly enough to be heard above the angry rhythm of the engine that was mounted close behind us, said, "We are out of balance and going down. We have to set down if we can find a spot."

When I had hooked the sling it was positioned so that as we lifted up part of it had looped over our right-hand landing skid. Gesturing toward a point of the mountain that jutted out into the canyon below us, I shouted, "There is a clearing on top of the saddle there."

He set us down smoothly.

I was quite chagrined as I climbed back in after adjusting the sling and I expected Don to be disgusted. He just smiled and twisted the throttle. The bird swung around and started to float up the side of that spectacular landscape like Aladdin's famous carpet. Twenty feet below us our cargo balanced perfectly. As we rose out of the shadows, we could see the whole mountain before us. It was a grand sight, and as the early morning sun with its special colors graced this rugged granite giant, I shouted, "Only a few people ever get to see this. Thank you, God—and you too, Don Landells."

Left to right: Ron Burch, Mike Donavan (who still flies for Landells Aviation), author and Clair Kunkel with the B3 helicopter used aerial prospecting. Photo by Vi Swan.

BRING A MECHANIC WITH YOU

It was another of those blazing hot summer days and as usual our spirit of adventure had replaced reason. Carl and I had spent the forepart of the day driving his old red Jeep (Lucifer) off into the trackless badlands to prospect. If there ever were any roads in the washes we were prowling, the annual summer cloudbursts had washed away any trace of them.

We had come across a gypsum bed, where the crystal forms of this ore looked like chunks of ice lying there in the sand. The sight was quite an anomaly since the ambient temperature was well over one hundred degrees Fahrenheit.

On our way back to Russell's camp we were quite content and were looking forward to cooling off in the shade of his trees, relaxing with a tall cool drink. I was driving and we were slowly making our way up Anvil Canyon Wash. Hot sand and a scattering of dry brown brush covered the steep upgrade. The air was still, hardly a rustle. Then the steady staccato of the four-cylinder Willis engine became more of a tapping sound and then that turned into a clatter. "Hey, Carl, what the heck?"

After throttling back the engine it still sounded awful. "Vell, we got to get to camp. Emmett, go ahead."

A few hundred feet farther the engine threw a connecting rod and we came to a most sudden stop. It was quiet, very quiet! Nothing was said. As the echo of the clattering engine died out in my brain there was just the occasional buzz of a fly and the crinkling of some metal parts of the Jeep reacting to a thermal summons.

Carl got out his side and I rolled out and we went around to the back and he started to dig into things and get out the tools and the jack. I grabbed a bucket and rummaged in my backpack and came up with a couple of pairs of cotton gloves. I believe it was quite some time before anything was said.

There was an occasional, "Ouch," or, "Damn it." as one of us would bump into some metal part of the sun baked Jeep. Carl drained the motor oil into the bucket and took the pan off. In the bottom of the pan we found the connecting rod bearing, twisted up like a crumpled piece of aluminum foil, and the rod cap along with the nuts that had once clamped everything together properly.

"Vell, we got to pull da cylinder head, too. Piston gone up too high and da top piston ring has locked up." I swallowed hard and nodded my head.

As we worked there was the illusion of relief from the sun as the Jeep slowly quit making noises, it's core settling to an even hot mass.

Off came the hood, which was set-aside over a small creosote bush. In a short time the head was off and the piston ring was compressed and back in place. Carl was careful not to disturb the head gasket any more than he had to. Ordinarily you never reuse any gaskets when you put an automobile engine back together because they will invariably leak and it is almost always a ticket to disaster. Carl, however, could fix anything mechanical; he was the best man to be with in this kind of a situation.

The repair went smoothly. Even those big horse flies that can bite right though your shirt stayed away, maybe because they didn't like the smell of the motor oil on us. Carl found some driftwood in the wash, chunks large enough for his purpose, and with a hammer he pounded the bearing back into a usable shape. In record time we had Lucifer reconstructed. As it was poised there in its oil stained sand wallow, engine purring again, we couldn't find any major leaks in the cooling system and no problem with the oil; good pressure—we congratulated ourselves and after sharing some hand cleaner and a rag we were on our way.

But there was a small moment when I held my breath and said to myself, "Dear God, how many times are you going to let us get away with a stunt like this?"

The sun was still high enough for us to appreciate the shade trees. The tall iced tea tasted ever so good.

BEWARE OF OLD INDIANS

In the northeast corner of Butte Valley there is a small cave. It is only 100 feet above one of the mine roads. In front of the cave is a bench formed of work chips. This terrace had been created by Native Americans. You don't need to be an archeologist to see that this site was used for hundreds of years for the manufacturing of weapons—knives, arrowheads, spear points and so forth. The cave is not much of a shelter and it can be described as two small adjoining rooms, both open on one side to the elements; shaded in the morning but open to the afternoon sun. Inside the ceiling is black from the smoke of innumerable fires.

Today the strategic location of this workstation that had been used for such a long period is not apparent. True, there was a trail that passed by in the wash below and there is a good view of the sloping alluvium to the west; however, now there is no sign of any spring or water source within miles. Another thing, none of the stock for these missile points seems to have come from anywhere around there.

I was standing in one of these rooms early one afternoon looking out over the upper end of Butte Valley, across the mesa area where I would often see large herds of wild burros grazing; or sometimes I would see a dramatic battle between jacks fighting for dominance. I stood there and began to wonder about the natives that had used this particular piece of real estate.

Above this Indian work chip cave is where I found the high-grade gold samples. The Smoke Jumpers are at the cave. Photo by author.

And the thought came to me that if I were here as a lookout, or working on arrow points, there would be a much better location directly above the openings. As I stepped out onto the pile of work chips there was that crunchy glass-like sound as the carpet of stone shifted. As I turned to face the hillside there appeared to be another ledge, just above the cave. I clambered around to the left through some boulders and when I was at the level above the ledge I looked down, startled! There before me was a work station with two flat-topped boulders side by side that had been used as work benches, and behind them were appropriate-sized stones to sit on. Work chips cluttered the floor of this open-air armory.

As I was sitting on one of the work stools it was easy to imagine that it was over a hundred years ago that someone else was in this same place looking down on the trail.

That was when the ghost of that old Indian came up behind me. All of a sudden I was prompted to look around to the left. There was another table-like rock to the side and on this rock someone had placed three brilliant stones, each the size of a plum. They were rich gold ore!

I could hear that old Indian laughing, as I thought, "Where in the hell do you suppose these came from?" Holding these mysterious gems in my hand, and maybe drooling a bit, I became angry at this joke. Clutching the three of them tightly, swinging my arm in a wide arc I threw them away—like any intelligent prospector would do with samples that were worthless because you had no idea where they came from. But you know what; my hand did not cooperate. When I opened my fist they were still there, haunting me, I hadn't been able to let go.

Oh, I spent an hour and covered a lot of the hill and found no trace of any formation that remotely resembled those ore samples. Today those three stones are in a dish on my desk. Sometimes when I look at them, I think I can hear that old Indian laughing at me.

IN THE DARK OF THE NIGHT, CIVET CATS

For those who are afraid of things that go bump in the night don't read this.

High up South Park Canyon, one evening, Harry Briggs and I were at the big table in his Banta Mill Site Camp. We had finished a long day, prospecting the steep rugged mountains nearby and after dinner we were relaxing. The only light in the large room, which served as kitchen, parlor, office and spare bedroom, was the whistling Coleman lantern in the center of the table. Its incandescent glow was limited, only adequate enough to fill a small area. Harry and I were sealed in by the darkness that filled most of the space around us.

Harry was in a talkative mood, and for once I was trying not to interrupt him. I had turned on my small tape recorder, and tilting back and balancing the sturdy chair on two legs, I listened. Today I can still relive this scene. On the tape I can hear Harry's voice, aged and happy, with a Midwest accent. There is the soft comforting music of the lantern and the staccato sounds of Harry managing his after-dinner smoke, often relighting his pipe, the sputtering of old kitchen matches, the occasional tapping of his favorite briar against the ashtray.

There was another sound, a sort of rustling somewhere off in the black veil. As he talked, Harry noticed me glancing about, turning a couple of times toward the east side of the room. "That's just the wind, that's all, Emmett." And he went on talking about his youth. A little while later, I thought I heard some more sounds, I was sure it wasn't the wind.

On into the evening, I gave in and I said, "Harry, excuse me, I think there is something over by your sink." I turned on the flashlight that had been lying on the table. The beam, pointed in the direction of the sound, illuminated several black-and-white spotted creatures about the size of an ordinary house cat. Being in the spotlight did not alarm them and that was sort of a relief, as it was obvious that our visitors were members of the skunk family. They were romping about, climbing in and out of the trash box by the sink.

Harry did not seem to be overly surprised either. When he saw them, he said, "Oh! There they are again." With the flashlight off, Harry went on telling me the story of his youth.

When we finally decided to call it a night, he retreated to a bed in a small room toward the rear of the building, and I was left to sleep on an old iron-framed bedstead that was against the wall across from the sink. There was a good distance between the bed and the trash can. I made my way across the room with some degree of trepidation, hoping the spotted creatures had already turned in. Pulling the bed away from the wall a bit I rolled out my sleeping bag, but before sleep came there was the sound of little feet racing around the floor.

I didn't risk making my way outside during the dark of the night. After my hurried trip out in the morning, I noticed that there was a house-cat door beside the main door and that there was debris scattered about this portal, inside and out, of the building. It appeared that our nocturnal prowlers used this little door readily. And inside their trail led right under the bed I had used. What a surprise when I bent down and looked underneath. There was a small-scale scene of death and destruction. Scattered around an opening in the inner wall were skeletons, claws, and skins of many little desert animals. It was no wonder there had been so much traffic during the night and now these carnivorous civet cats (as some people called this kind of a skunk) were snug asleep in their cozy home inside the wall.

Harry was somewhat disappointed to find he was their landlord, but he was even more disappointed in their poor manners. He explained that he had been rudely awakened when one of them jumped up onto his bed that night. He explained, "That's never happened before. I guess I gotta do something."

After I was gone he had set about to solve the problem. He told me, "I set up a 30-gallon barrel and put bait inside. After the bunch of them were attacking the bait I slipped a lid over the barrel and filled it with water. That drowned them without them raising their tails at me and smellin' up the place."

When he told me this, I could not help but show him how much I knew about skunks. "Harry, down where my house is in the San Bernardino Mountains I've met some people that trap skunks and they told me that if you use a low trap so that the skunks can't raise their tail they can't use their spray apparatus. Also they told me that if you shot one in the head so that it died instantly there wouldn't be any smell either."

The next time I met him, Harry said, "Emmett you're right about those pole cats. I was down at my Redlands camp, talking to some people, sitting at my big desk, ya know, and I opened one of them side drawers and there was one, big as life. Well, I opened the top drawer and got my pistol. I shot him clean as could be, no problem!"

I have often wondered how startled the people he had been talking to had been when he had demonstrated how to safely get rid of a skunk.

JACOB WALTZ, DON'T SHOW HIM YOUR GOLD

Drawn to the Dutchman's story like a magnet is drawn to metal, it was necessary for me to learn as much as I could about this man. His is the most famous lost mine story in the world. There have been books, and more books, about it, published in many languages all over the globe. When I was older and had the opportunity I went to Arizona's Sonoran Desert and walked through those same forbidding Superstition Mountains where he had been.

The Dutchman was not the figment of some writer's dream. He had been a typical western prospector and he finally ended up in Phoenix, Arizona. He had become a naturalized U.S. citizen in Los Angeles, California in 1861 on July 19, an immigrant from Prussia. There are many who have seen some of the super–rich specimens of gold-laced quartz that he had brought back from the Superstition Mountains thirty miles east of Phoenix. After he died in 1891 there is record of a legal fight over a box of gold ore that had been under his deathbed; several people had claimed he had promised them the gold. Julia Thomas was a neighbor of Jacob's and had given him refuge after a great flood of the Salt River had washed his house away and left him an invalid. She started the unending search for the mine in 1893, as reported in *The Arizona Weekly Gazette*, when she sold her business in Phoenix, bought an outfit, and disappeared with a couple of companions for two months into the forbidden (sacred to the local Apache Indians) mountain range. Julia didn't find Jacob's mine but she came back to publicly claim that Jacob had bequeathed his secret mine to her, telling her and her boyfriend how to find it the night before he died (she didn't tell about the firewater she and her boyfriend consumed that evening that may have clouded the memory of the directions he gave them.) Since then, over twenty persons have either died or been murdered in the Superstition Mountains trying to find where Jacob's mine was, and the legend has it that Jacob was not the first to gather the gleaming ore from this spot. The story says that he murdered the Mexicans that had it before him and kept its location secret with subsequent murders.

A man who knew Jacob, told that the old man had confessed to him that he had murdered three men in order to get the mine. Reportedly the tale went something like this. "I was traveling from one mining camp to another and went into the mountains using the old military trail that was used by the soldiers as a route from Fort McDowell on the Verde River to Camp Pinal, near the head of Queen Creek."

The reader here needs to picture the Sonoran Desert. It is much different—more verdant than the Mojave. In the isolated mountains where he was it is almost semitropical, thick brush, trees, and the giant saguaro cactus.

To continue Jacob's narrative: "Toward nightfall I caught a glimpse of four Apache Indians who were waiting to ambush me. I turned and ran off into the brush. The Apaches were close behind, and I ran for hours in darkness. By morning I had gotten away from them—I was lost, exhausted and out of water. I had abandoned all of my gear. In a wash I discovered some footprints that were not made by Indians. I stumbled on, following their tracks until I came to a deserted camp. There was plenty of food and water, and I helped myself greedily and soon fell sound asleep. In the late afternoon I was awakened by three Mexicans when they returned to their camp. They welcomed me and made me comfortable. The next day they invited me to accompany them to their mine. They were mining the richest gold ore I had ever seen and they were proud to show me their success. During the day I went back to camp with one of the men. When I had a chance, I shot him. When the other two Mexicans came into the camp, I shot them."

❋

And so back to our Death Valley. The ghosts here live on, too. This sanctuary, this desert, will always be a land of long shadows, fragrant delicate vapors, and every remote hard-to-get-to place may be hiding something! There will be burning sand and lonely cold nights. Days so wonderfully filled with tranquility. Silence, peace—however, always beware. Even with the most modern equipment available for those that are brave enough to wander the "wasteland"; they should never underestimate this prodigy, it will always surprise you. There will be no prelude, not like the movies.

If you go into this wonderland, BE PREPARED NOT ONLY TO ENJOY ITS BEAUTY, BUT BE READY TO EMBRACE THE SPIRIT OF THE OLD WEST; IT IS STILL PART OF THE VALLEY!

EPILOGUE

The desert phenomenon, known today as Death Valley National Park California, existed of course long before modern man. It has had many names. Many of the different societies that have lived or visited there for thousands of years have assumed jurisdiction.

At this time, it has never had so large and diversified a population. Many people are enjoying its worldwide allure. The park has become a great attraction, popular with travel agencies all over the world. I have been surprised, when I am in the valley now, most of the people that I meet are not from this country, and these foreigners have a much more positive outlook about the valley than do local Californians or other close neighbors.

As close as Los Angeles, California, locals think that the valley is a terrible place, a place to be avoided. Too harsh, too warm. They will consider the possibility of visiting Scotty's Castle there, but maybe in the winter. A couple of years ago, during the summer, when I told people in my office that I was going to take off and go to the valley to work on a story about four missing German tourists, I was considered out of my mind. They said that the valley would be a terrible place—inhospitable in the summer. However when I met Brita Marks (an investigating reporter from Hamburg, Germany) a few days later at Furnace Creek Ranch Resort, in the heart of the valley, we were anything but uncomfortable. Our cool, tree-shaded air-conditioned rooms faced a large swimming pool that was accessible through sliding glass doors. All of the tourists we met on that visit were from some other country, mostly Germany; all of them were having a wonderful holiday. Even the employees at the resorts in the valley are often new immigrants.

When more recently Ruth and I were with Cliff and Barbara Walker at Stovepipe Wells Village, leading an expedition of students, the room clerk in the office at the motel had only been in this country two weeks. She told me that in fact, she was a new bride, a mail-order bride from Russia. When I asked her how she

Recent picture of the author and his wife Ruth above South Park Canyon overlooking Striped Butte Valley. Photo by Cliff Walker.

had learned to speak English so well she said, "I studied English at the university." I might add that she was "bubbling-over" with cheerfulness, and she was remarkably competent.

The administrators of the park tell me that the number of foreign tourists vacationing in the valley increases, many thousands, each year.

Death Valley still can be very dangerous. The four tourists, who haven't been found yet, disappeared in the same area that this book covers. Their disabled van was found at a place in Anvil Canyon where our Jeep once broke down. Ruth and I were more fortunate when I was able to make repairs, and we did not have three flat tires as their car did. In December this year a geology student from Washington State, Gabriel Cisneros, found the skeleton of a man (with a variety of twenty dollar bills scattered about) two miles from the nearest road. As of this writing no one has discovered who this man was or how he came to be there (Inyo County Sheriff's Investigator Jim Jones). The modern Nike hiking shoes found with the bleached bones demonstrates that the valley can still be dangerous.

There was a shoot-out incident in the valley last year; it was a modern affair, a car chase (the bad guys and a girl in a Mercedes) and it ended up on a dry lake not far from the park headquarters. Oh, yes, a police helicopter damaged by gunfire had to make an emergency landing. The three miscreants, who were armed with a variety of military assault weapons, were subdued after they ran out of water.

When you visit, enjoy, but follow the ample advice supplied by the Park Service. As always, be careful.

INDEX

ABOUT THE AUTHOR

Emmett Harder could be called the real "Indiana Jones", no movie double, he has had many unconventional opportunities. Born during the 1930's economic depressions. He grew up as a latch-key child through the 1940's, while his father and mother and his four older brothers were caught up in the nation's WWII war effort. Even before his life was interrupted to take part in the Korean conflict, and he was sent on a clandestine attempt to save the French at Dien Bien Phu, in what later became the Vietnam war, he was out prowling the great desert. Having traveled to many far away places and worked on a variety of projects, he still says, "I feel most at home in the wastelands of Death Valley. I have always been a child of the desert, starting at 14-years-old and dragging my 11-year-old brother with me. And like the old prospector in the "Treasure of The Sierra Madre" story, I'm still out there looking for the next strike."

Emmett is a writer, lecturer, historian and researcher. He teaches at Cal State University San Bernardino's Extended Education Division. Often he leads organized safaris into historic and mysterious places. As a reader at the Huntington Research Library, with his unique understanding of how things really happen, he is often lost in the distant adventures.

When I asked him why he wrote this book, he said,

"I guess I'm like most people, a treasure hunter and adventurer at heart.

"But because I was born while there were still stories and treasures in '*them thar hills*' I was lucky enough to stumble into more than my share of both."

He went on to say, "Not too long ago, another prospector from that same era, Earl Fox, and I were in a remote canyon in Death Valley (South Park Canyon) looking at a very narrow seam of quartz. It ran for a ways along one of the sheer massive granite walls that crowded out most of the sunlight. Of course quartz is a most common thing but here there was a very thin trace of gold in this white glass-like stratum.

"Earl had stopped the Jeep to show me this curiosity. We had walked a short distance through the rock debris left from the last cloudburst to look at it. He said, 'Harry Briggs showed this to me years ago.' The mention of Mr. Briggs brought on a flood of memories. We sat back in the shade on a couple of boulders and started talking about all the people that we had crossed trails with, that, like Harry, were gone now—Carl Ruona, Will Roper, Billy Myers, Asa Russell—and the list went on and on.

"There we were in this imposing natural granite tomb and as the minutes passed, in my mind, I could see each of these desert wanderers. I felt the presence of all of these old-timers, finally I blurted out, 'Earl, these canyons are full of ghosts!'

"Later, when my wife insisted that I take time out from writing other adventure stories and write about my own odyssey in Death Valley—and when she and Tom and Alice Cullbertson asked me what the title of this book would be—again I didn't hesitate, I said, *These Canyons Are Full of Ghosts*." —Cliff Walker

——— NOTES ———